THE

HOMEWARD PATH.

BY THE AUTHOR OF

"THE BEGINNING AND GROWTH OF THE CHRISTIAN LIFE, OR THE SUNDAY-SCHOOL TEACHER."

"Blessed are they that do His commandments, that they may have right to the tree of life, and may enter in through the gates into the city."

THIRD EDITION.

BOSTON:
WALKER, WISE, AND COMPANY,
245 WASHINGTON STREET.
1860.

University Press, Cambridge:
Welch, Bigelow, & Co., Electrotypers and Printers.

CONTENTS.

LETTER I.

INTRODUCTORY.

The interest I have long felt in you, my young friend, has led me to form the purpose of addressing to you a series of letters, relative to your inward life, your spiritual needs, and your Christian growth and progress. Novelty of thought or illustration will not be my aim, but to aid you in the attainment of that secret life which is "hid with Christ in God."

From my acquaintance with the influences that immediately surround you, I have thought there might be times when you earnestly longed to express your feelings and wants to some heart in which you could place confidence, and find the sympathy and help you secretly crave. Either repressed by personal diffidence, or repulsed by the reserve or coldness of others, or by a secret consciousness that your deepest wants and spiritual difficulties would not be understood by those around you, you have passed on from month to month, sometimes feeling that you had gained a little in the true path, — sometimes wholly discouraged, — often indifferent, and with little or no definite aim in your spiritual life. Sometimes you have felt a sort of pride in hiding your better feelings under the mask of coldness or indifference; sometimes, by a frivolous manner, or a light, careless word, you have sought to conceal those secret convictions that would not let you rest in complacent ease and self-satisfaction; and sometimes, too, you have sincerely and earnestly longed for some true Christian friend to whom you might express your dissatisfaction and your secret anxiety, — some one who would truly sympathize with you and aid you.

To meet such longings, to supply so far as I may the place of a personal counsellor and friend, to lead you to a better understanding of your true position, of your personal relation to God and to Christ, and to point out to you your only true path of life, in a child-like obedience and a Christian faith and trust, will be my single and sincere endeavor.

If at any time my words may not seem applicable to your immediate state of mind, your own judgment will point out the true course of thought and inquiry; remembering that, while the great facts of a spiritual experience are ever one and the same, they are also modified according to the peculiar mental habits, native dispositions, and natural temperament of the individual.

Let me beg you, then, not to adopt my conclusions, or to trust my guidance alone ; but by a prayerful study of the Word of Truth, as applicable to your own heart and character, may you be led to the one only living Fountain of Life and Peace.

LETTER II

INWARD DISSATISFACTION AND UNEASINESS.

The state of your mind, my dear friend, as revealed in your welcome letter, is probably not so strange and peculiar as you seem to imagine; for the same restlessness, the same dissatisfaction, the same uneasy longings and disquiets, the same anxious fears and trembling hopes, have, in some form, been felt by every soul that has been roused, even for a little season, to a sense of its spiritual needs.

Unless the child has been educated under the purest Christian influences, and in early youth has given the heart to God and to Christ, — unless the new birth into the spiritual life, the birth of the immortal desires and affections, has been simultaneous with the growth and development of that which is merely earthly and perishable, — the season must come when questions such as these force themselves upon the soul with irresistible power: — "What am I, and whither do I tend? For what purpose am I living? What is my trust for the present, and what my only true hope for the future? Have I any sure foundation of faith? Know I, from experience, aught of that life over which death hath no power? Do I *really* believe in God, in Christ, in immortality? What is the meaning of salvation through Christ, and of the kingdom of heaven being within?"

No matter how pure and fair the life to outward seeming, no matter what has been the judgment of partial friends or careless observers, if the soul is not conscious of a *personal* interest in divine things, if it feels that it is not one with Christ, and through him reconciled to the Father, if it knows nothing from its own experience of the love of a Saviour, and of the Divine holiness and compassion manifested in and through him, then must there be discontent, dissatisfaction, uneasiness. Be sure there is that within you which will make you restless, and which *must* make you restless, until you find rest in God. Through a personal acceptance of the Redeemer alone, will you find peace.

But you say: "I do long, and at times earnestly long, for a more consistent, purer, higher life than I am now leading. What is merely outward does not and cannot satisfy me. Health, friends, the comforts of life, intellectual pursuits, the stimulus of conscious mental progress, the rewards of faithful industry, — all such blessings are no unworthy sources of happiness; yet in seasons of any peculiar trial or temptation, or in hours of solitude and self-recollection, I find they utterly fail me. There is a deeper life concealed from human view, of which at such times I am conscious; there are wants which the common occupations or pleasures or intercourse of the day do not and cannot satisfy.

"I turn to the pages of the New Testament, and as I read there the glowing words of the Apostles, expressive of a living faith in Christ, of a love stronger than death, of a love that casteth out all fear,—as I hear them speak of a life hid with Christ in God, of longing to depart and to be with Christ,—I feel that I have not yet learned even the alphabet of religious truth. I believe in Christ, that is, intellectually I believe in him; but I do not feel my personal relation to him as a Saviour and Redeemer. I admire the purity of his life; I see something of the greatness of his mission, and reverence his self-sacrificing love, and the tenderness of his compassion; but when he speaks of himself as the only 'Way, Truth, and Life,'—when he says, 'No man cometh unto the Father but by me,' 'I am the Resurrection and the Life,'—when the Apostle emphatically declares of Christ, that there is no other name under heaven, given among men, whereby we can be saved,—I feel that there is a meaning in such words which I have not yet begun to fathom, — a sense in which he is the Saviour of man of which as yet I know nothing.

"Sometimes I have tried to dissipate these thoughts by outward excitement, sometimes by a more stringent performance of duty; but in a few days I have yielded to old habits and delinquencies, feeling how mechanical was such a routine.

"I make resolves to govern my passions, to curb my wayward temper, to be more faithful to my daily duties and my obligations to others; but again and again do I break them, and I am weary of striving. The ground I think I have gained, in a few days of relaxed watchfulness and of discontent is entirely lost, and the same resolves are made, week after week, only to meet with the same results.

"I look to the pure and noble examples of some whom I reverence and love, and as I know their calmness, nay, even joy of spirit, amid trial and sorrow, their peace of mind amid the petty vexations of daily life, I feel that theirs is a hidden source of strength and repose which, as yet, I have not found. Often, too, when I strive to pray, there seems no reality in the service. God seems afar off, and retribution and immortality and heaven mere dreams. I repeat the Saviour's own words, but his being and presence are too often vague and shadowy; I do not feel my personal relationship to him, nor my indebtedness to him, and his commands possess little abiding control over my inward being. I am dissatisfied and inwardly restless. I am conscious of yearning desires that are not satisfied, of aspirations that are not filled. The future often looks to me uncertain, mysterious, and dark, and there are moments when, with all that to the world's eye seems bright and fair, life appears to me scarcely desirable.

"Is there indeed a reality in the Christian faith, a peace and a hope which the world gives not, and cannot take away? Are these thoughts and questionings, these vague surmises, these anxious longings and desires, these hours of dissatisfaction and self-reproach, mere fanciful chimeras? And if not, how am I to meet them, — how find light and peace for the soul?"

No, my young friend; thoughts and questionings like these are no mere fancies, no vain delusions of the soul, but the voice of the Spirit pleading with you, striving with you, to turn you from the fading glitter of earthly trifles and passing pursuits, from vain attempts at self-excitation and mere self-culture, and to repose your weary, restless heart on the bosom of Infinite Pity and Love. God would have you to be wholly his, and to find your true peace only through the mediation and love of Christ. And so he would teach you by all this inward dissatisfaction and uneasiness that the earth is not your abiding-place, nor this world your home; that there is but one path in which you are to walk, — the path of humble self-consecration and devotion to his service; that there is but one guide whom you are to follow, — even Him who is the very manifestation of the Father.

Thank God that in any measure you have begun to feel your spiritual necessities; that the voice of the Spirit has been heard within your soul; that, however dim the inward light, you yet do long, and long earnestly at times, for a deeper faith, a warmer love, and a better life.

Cherish these feelings, I entreat you, — cherish them more than the most costly of jewels, — for they are the strivings of your immortal nature, the voice of that within which cannot die, the pleadings of that Holy Spirit which, in times past, you have so often grieved away by your thoughtlessness or passion or frivolity, or by your undue absorption in the outward, transient pursuits of life.

Pray, too, however dim your faith, however unrealizing to your soul may be the being and the presence of God. Pray through Christ, that you may be taught *how* to pray. Neglect not this exercise, unless you would lose at once all higher aspirations and aims; neglect it not, however little present help or comfort you may seem to derive from it; neglect it not, at the peril of your own soul. "Draw nigh to God," however feebly, however imperfectly, and "he will draw nigh to you." "Seek, and ye shall find."

In your present state of mind, everything depends upon your fidelity to this duty. Neglect it, and indifference, worldliness, and carelessness will again roll back their dark and heavy waves over your soul, and perhaps never again will you hear, as now, that heavenly voice which says to you, "Arise, and depart, for this is not your rest." Neglect it, and perchance the solemn realities of an opening eternity shall first again awaken you from your deathlike slumber of cold indifference.

"Return, O wanderer, now return,
And seek thy Father's face;
Those new desires which in thee burn
Were kindled by his grace.

"Return, O wanderer, now return,
And wipe the falling tear;
The Spirit calls, — no longer mourn,
'T is Love invites thee near."

LETTER III.

ALIENATION FROM GOD.

The first step, my young friend, which you need to take, is to understand more clearly your true state of mind, and the causes of your present dissatisfaction and anxieties. Let me, then, say distinctly and emphatically, that all of your spiritual troubles and mental difficulties proceed from one fruitful source of uneasiness and disquiet, — the alienation of your soul from God, — the evil and the sin that is within. I do not now undertake to discuss the cause of this unhappy state, or to inquire what is the true origin of it. Theories on this subject are as numerous as leaves in the forest, and to discuss them or theorize concerning them here would be of no avail, even were it possible for the age-long question to be settled; for peace rarely, if ever, comes through a mere intellectual conviction. Enough that you feel the want within, that you know the sin to be there, that you are conscious of this bitter sense of alienation from your God and Father, that you long, in your better moments, for light, faith, reconciliation.

And now what you need is to deepen within you, by prayer and meditation, this sense of inward destitution, until your whole soul is filled with the longing desire for relief; until your one earnest and heartfelt prayer is for that repentance that needeth not to be repented of, — for that pardon so freely vouchsafed, through Christ, to every penitent, humble soul.

Could you once feel that your will was God's will, your purposes and desires one with his, that you were his child, and that everything which befalls you on your pilgrimage, every circumstance of your changing life, is ordered by his perfect wisdom and love, you would no longer restlessly fret against your daily surroundings, or say to yourself that a different position would impart what you inwardly need; for there would be in the soul itself the repose and trust of the little child in its Father's home, — and would not such a trust be happiness?

Hitherto, the circumstances of your outward life have, in some measure, concealed from you your true character, especially as you have but recently contemplated your inner life with that close and searching scrutiny which the question, "How far have I any claim to the Christian name?" ever demands.

Your lot thus far has been comparatively a sheltered one. In the sanctuary of home the fiercer temptations have not assailed you. You have not been called to test the strength of your principles or your power of resistance by conflict with the sternest and most bitter forms of human trial. You have enjoyed many religious privileges in the instructions of the Church, and from your earliest years the Scriptures have been within your reach. You have often chosen and done the right, but you now feel that this was the result rather of mere external influences, than of any firm, deliberate choice in the soul. Your faith has been that of the intellect, not of the heart. You have made resolves, planned duties, and sought, for a time, zealously to fulfil them, but have often failed, because you have relied on your own strength alone. You have sometimes engaged in works of benevolence, and have doubtless done something to alleviate the sorrows and sufferings of others; but even such works have afforded no abiding satisfaction, for often they have been engaged in with far too much of self-reference, rather than in the simple desire to follow in the Master's steps, — with a feeling as if by the performance of such duties you were earning a title to self-approval. You have believed in God, that is, you have said to yourself that you believed in him as an all-wise and holy Creator; but you have not lived as in the presence of a Father, encompassing your whole path, reading each secret thought, watching each flitting desire, and answering each true and heavenward aspiration, — a God of holiness not to be trifled with, a God of justice not to be gainsaid, a God of love desiring nothing so much as that every child of his should be righteous and safe.

You have spoken in general terms of Christ as the Saviour of the world; but you have not felt your personal indebtedness to him, your personal need of him, as the only Reconciler of the soul to God. Your thoughts have often rested on the future; but there has been too little keenness of spiritual perception for you to cherish, hitherto, much, if any, doubt as to your acceptance with God. You have thought your situation safe because you evinced an outward respect for religion, were guilty of no flagrant sins, and bore, to the world's eye, a correct moral character. But you now feel that such a state of mind is far from being a right, safe, or Christian state, and ask: "How shall I render my present dissatisfaction the means of true repentance and of spiritual growth? What is my first duty? How shall I attain to a realizing Christian faith?"

I reply: First of all, study the Scriptures with a direct, personal reference to your own wants, desires, and needs. Study them now, not for intellectual knowledge, not for criticism, but as the direct revelation of God's will and law to your own soul, as containing your only true standard of judgment, your only chart and inspiration.

Read the Sermon on the Mount, and apply its divine precepts, one by one, to your own feelings, words, habits, and dispositions, so that you may see how far your inward life accords with its high standard, as manifested in the life of the Redeemer.

"Blessed are the *pure in heart*," the humble, the meek, the forgiving, the forbearing; "blessed are they who hunger and thirst after righteousness," not with a faint longing, an indefinite desire, a vague aspiration, but with an earnest, hearty, whole-souled seeking after purity and holiness. "Judge not, that ye be not judged; forgive, as ye would be forgiven; as ye would that men should do to you, do ye even so to them," — in kindness, gentleness, sympathy, forbearance, charity.

Does your past life bear witness to fidelity even in these simple requirements? But you are bidden to take up the cross daily, and follow Christ; to follow him in his self-renunciation, his self-sacrificing love, his devotion to God, his love to man. Is such your case? Have you begun resolutely and in earnest to lead such a life?

Read and ponder those last sublime discourses of the Saviour with his disciples; and as you meditate on that love stronger than death, as you listen to his earnest words of affectionate entreaty and promise, "Abide in me, and I in you;

I will not leave you comfortless, I will come unto you," ask yourself, — if you know from personal experience the blessed reality of those words, — how far your outward life has been the result of this close, intimate relation of your soul to that of the Redeemer. Meditate, too, on the perfect holiness of God, and the requirements of his law, until you understand more truly what sin is; how abhorent in the sight of Infinite Purity, how hateful in view of Perfect Holiness! Meditate upon it until you deeply feel that the state of alienation from God in which you have been contented to live, the coldness and indifference which have characterized so much of your past life, are in themselves sins of fearful moment.

Living beneath the eye of the greatest and holiest of beings, enjoying every moment blessings from his hand more than you can recount, depending upon his watchful love and guardian care for every breath you draw, upon the inworking of his ever-present Spirit for every power of mind you exercise, upon his tender mercy, vouchsafing to you so many sources of the purest happiness through the exercise of your kindly affections, — you have yet been content to pass days and weeks and months, as if all of these things depended only on the exercise of your own strength, as if they were rightfully your own, and derived from your own powers alone. These uncounted, infinite favors of the

Holy One you have received as a mere matter of course, with no thought of the Giver, no grateful recognition of the hand that strews your daily path with blessings. From day to day, you have enjoyed the rich bounties of his kind providence, forgetting Him in whom alone you live and move, and have your whole being. Is not such ingratitude sin? How often, too, have your seasons of devotion been either wholly neglected, or hurried through, because some engagement was to be fulfilled, some pleasure to be enjoyed, some recitation to be prepared, or some business to be accomplished, too important to be postponed! But have you ever questioned the relative importance of these things in the sight of God?

How often have you entered upon the untried scenes of a new day, refreshed by peaceful slumber, and renovated in every faculty, without one ascription of praise and thanksgiving, one petition for heavenly strength, guidance, and protection! And when the duties and cares and enjoyments of the day have closed, how often have you yielded your powers to the calm insensibility of repose, without one thought of Him who compasses your path and your lying down, who besets you behind and before, and even lays his hand upon you in infinite and tender compassion, that you may turn and look to him!

This forgetfulness of God, — this cold indifference, — is not this sin? A child to forget his parent, — to live in the Father's house, unmindful of the Father's presence, — is it not strange, unnatural, sinful?

But you say, or rather you have often secretly felt, that God was altogether too merciful to call you to any stringent account for your failures or short-comings; that he would never exercise any retributive justice upon a character on the whole so moral and correct as your own. Taking the sublime revelation, that God is Love, and making it a sort of covert for your low aims and unspiritual purposes, you have never fathomed its deep and vast significance, nor remembered that justice is a part of love, and that perfect holiness is an essential attribute of the Almighty. The fear of the Lord is the beginning of wisdom; and because you know so little of the Divine attributes, you have felt as if all were well with you, forgetting that Immaculate Purity, before which the very heavens are not clean.

This deep sense of the Divine holiness, of the strict requirements of his law, and of your own sins, omissions, and short-comings, can alone lead you to feel your personal need of the Saviour. You may admire his example, you may wonder at his miracles, you may rejoice in his acts of beneficence, you may weep over his sufferings, or exult in his glory; but you will not enter into tender sympathy or loving communion with him, until you are brought to feel a *personal* interest in his spirit; until you feel your need of one who shall assure you of pardon and reconciliation, of one in whose strength your weakness shall find support, of one in whose compassionate regard and affection the secret yearnings of your soul shall alone be satisfied. After all your indifference, forgetfulness, and negligence, the dark background of conscious sin, unworthiness, and alienation from God must first display the radiant image of the cross.

You reply, that you do believe in the law of God, that you wish to feel thus, and that, at times, you truly desire to love Christ and to be his disciple; but you are so often utterly indifferent, the truths of religion seem so unreal, that you cannot grasp them, nor give them in your mind the weight which you know belongs to them.

Such feelings are the necessary result of much of your past unfaithfulness and negligence; of having often grieved away the Spirit, and closed your heart to the pleadings of the Divine voice. But I earnestly entreat you, look no longer to anything outward as the cause of your present disquiet. The difficulty is within. The evil is there alone. God's voice is again speaking to you. Quench not the Spirit. Listen to its monitions, and may it guide you to Christ, the Way and the Life.

"My Father bids me come;
O, why do I delay?
He calls my wandering spirit home,
And yet from him I stay.

"Father, the hindrance show
Which I have failed to see;
And let me now consent to know
What keeps me far from thee.

"In me the hindrance lies; —
The fatal bar remove,
And let me see, in sweet surprise,
Thy full redeeming love."

LETTER IV.

NEED OF RECONCILIATION, AND OF A DISTINCT RELIGIOUS CHOICE.

You feel, my dear friend, and truly feel, that your character is not all that it should be, that your faith is that of the intellect rather than of the heart, subject to the fluctuations of each passing emotion or opinion, or changing outward scene. You read, and now at length ponder for yourself the solemn words of Christ, "Except a man be born again, he cannot enter into the kingdom of Heaven," and you feel that, however fair your character may stand in the eyes of others, there has not been, deep in your soul, the firm, deliberate choice of Christ as your only Guide and Saviour, that the ruling desire and aim of your spirit has not been that of a child-like obedience to the Father. You know that

> "The world can never give
> The bliss for which you sigh,"

that neither outward success, nor luxurious living, nor intellectual attainments, nor engrossment in business or pleasure, nor even the diligent dis charge of external duties alone, can ever fill those profound inward cravings of the spirit; and you ask, "How can I more deeply feel and realize my wants, and know my only true position, so as to be able firmly and deliberately to resolve, 'Henceforth, Jesus shall be my only guide; I *will* strive, God helping me, to be a true and faithful disciple'?"

I reply, Next to that personal study and application of the truths of Scripture of which I have already spoken, seek frequent and prolonged seasons of meditation and communion with your God and your Saviour. Seek the hour of retirement. Look carefully and searchingly within, and again and again meditate on the great facts of your inward life, until they become more real and true than aught in the outward world of passing events, — until they become the reality, the outward only the shadow.

Remember that there are two opposing forces in the world, to either of which you may yield allegiance as the governing principle of your life,—two conflicting tendencies within you, the one leading you upward to God, to truth, to heaven, through all that is pure and holy and benevolent and good; the other dragging you down to evil and loss and perdition, through indifference and selfishness, frivolity and sensual indulgence, and a life without God in the world. You cannot equally divide your affections and allegiance. You cannot serve God and Mammon. You cannot be a disciple of Christ and a votary of business or fashion. You cannot love the Father and love the world. One principle or the other must reign supreme. Neutrality is impossible, or a life equally balanced between the two. We cannot follow Christ when it is pleasant, and our own inclinations when his law and example would bid us deny self, and take up the cross and follow him. There must be in the soul a solemn, deliberate choice, guiding the whole character and life. Outward morality cannot take the place of inward piety, nor self-culture that of a true, upward-looking faith in God through Christ.

Your present discontent and restlessness is the necessary result of past unfaithfulness, and you need heartfelt penitence, not merely for single acts of wrong, but for the whole disobedient temper and alienated heart.

Different persons may call such feelings, such needs, by different names, but the fact is none the less true and real. You may term it conviction of sin, renewal, the second birth, reconciliation, harmony with God, a true faith,— yet the meaning is one and the same. It is the need of feeling one's self in friendship with God, the need of pardon and reconciliation, the assurance that henceforth you hold the position of a true child to the Father, whom he implicitly trusts and loves, — that your will and desires and purposes are one with his. There are those who hide such convictions under the delusive mask of gayety, frivolity, or absorption in business or pleasure ; and if they deny their reality, it is because they have never looked into the hidden mysteries of the soul or listened to its deep self-questionings, so far as to be conscious of their real wants. But the fact is clearly before us, mirrored in weary hearts, in restless spirits, in dissatisfied, unhappy minds, all the world over.

It was this consciousness of inward need, more than aught else, that drew the disciples around the Master; for they felt that in him the soul's secret longings would find satisfaction and peace. It was this that brought the humbled penitent to his feet; that led the gentle Mary to listen with such grateful love to every word that fell from his divine lips ; that led Nicodemus to seek him, amid the covert shades and stillness of the night; that brought the wearied, the sick, and the heavy-laden to seek were it but one word of assurance and pardon, one word of heavenly authority, saying, " Come unto me, and I will give you rest."

Paul needed it, with all his eloquence, ere he became a humble disciple in the school of Christ. The jailer at Philippi needed it, when he cried out in his agony and fear, " What must I do to be saved? Agrippa needed it, as, enthroned in royal state, he coldly cast aside the golden opportunity, and to the eloquent and persuasive pleadings of his noble prisoner mockingly exclaimed, " Almost thou persuadest me to be a Christian." Loyola needed it, when stretched on the couch of anguish and suffering, as the pomps and glories of the outward world faded from his view, and the solemn realities of the spirit life startled his slumbering conscience with a power too mighty and too authoritative to be gainsaid. Bunyan needed it, until he commenced to verify in his own strange and eventful life his " Pilgrim's Progress " to a better land. The accomplished Chalmers needed it, ere he learned the lesson of an entire self-renunciation, ere the seal of an inward consecration had sanctified his noble powers to the Master's use.

You too have felt the need, amid the engrossing duties of your school life, the excitements and joys of opening youth, the trials and pleasures of home duties, beneath the pressure of care, or in anxious watchings by the sick-bed, or in hours of bodily pain and weariness, or of solitude and loneliness. And be assured that unless you utterly stifle your better convictions, and quench the pleadings of the Spirit, you *will* feel it, until you seek the only relief in sincere penitence, and a deliberate choice, as to the guide, the Master you will serve, — leading you to a sincere Christian faith.

> " I feel within a want,
> For ever burning there ; —
> What I so thirst for, grant,
> O Thou who hearest prayer ! "

But you are not left alone in making this choice. God is already working within you by his Spirit, both to will and to do of his good pleasure. " No man," says the Saviour, " can come to me," can even desire or wish to come, " unless the Father who hath sent me draw him." And now it is your part to open your heart freely and fully to these divine influences, — to seek in earnest and persevering prayer the help, the strength, the peace you need.

Be true to your own soul. Let nothing interrupt your daily seasons of devotion. Seek truly the constant help of the Spirit ; and let me again and earnestly entreat you not to neglect this duty *because* you feel cold or indifferent, or to say to yourself that in such a state of mind prayer would be a mockery. Only the more because of such feelings is it your duty. It is God's appointed and commanded means of gaining the strength, the faith you need. And he has never promised to give you the best desires of your heart, the best gifts of his grace, unless you *seek* and *ask* for them. Go to him, then, in your coldness and indifference ; go, that you may receive of his light and life. If at times you feel utterly indifferent, only say, " Lord, teach me to pray; give me the *desire* to pray"; and let this single petition dwell in your heart, and rise again and again in your thoughts, until a better desire dawn, and you can again offer the sincere prayer for forgiveness and strength. You *know* that there is only loss and danger to the soul in absenting yourself from the mercy-seat. It is not then a mockery to come, even when you are cold and indifferent. It is to come to your Father,—to come, just as the little child goes to his earthly parent, with all his griefs and his joys, knowing that he will find help and sympathy and love.

> "Be constant at the throne of grace,
> And *persevere* in prayer."

Remember, too, the words of promise, "If ye, being evil, know how to give good gifts unto your children, how much more shall your Father who is in heaven give the Holy Spirit to them that ask him." "Likewise the Spirit also helpeth our infirmities; for we know not what we should pray for as we ought; but the Spirit itself maketh intercession for us with groanings which cannot be uttered."

Expect not always to feel the same interest and the same fervor; but having striven, by reflection and serious meditation, to awaken in your soul a sense of the Divine Presence and of your own wants and needs, then hesitate no longer; and however imperfect, however brief, the prayer thus offered will never fail of its answer in God's own time and way.

Make then your choice firmly and deliberately; say to yourself, "I am determined henceforth to be a disciple of Christ; I know in my better moments the infinite importance of spiritual realities; I know the unsatisfactory nature of all mere earthly pursuits, and I am determined to choose Him for my Guide and Friend who will never fail me, who so lovingly invites me to come to him."

You will often fail; you will daily fall short of your resolves; you will still have to struggle with feelings of indifference and apathy; but there will be deep in your soul this consciousness: "I have resolved, before God, to *strive* to be his child. I will no longer live as an alien from my Father's house. I will come back, and whatever discipline of sorrow or trial he may appoint, I will receive it gratefully, as a means of leading me nearer to himself";—

> "For now my spirit sighs for home,
> And longs for light whereby to see,
> And like a weary child would come,
> O Father, unto Thee!"

Is not such a deliberate choice, such a simple resolve, possible? Does it not now depend wholly on yourself, and does not God require it of you? The Spirit is again pleading with you. Grieve it not away. Give up everything, rather than quench its influences; for "*now* is the accepted time." It may be that your whole future well-being will depend upon the faithful use you make of your present convictions, of the present consciousness of your wants and needs. To stand still is to go back; for light will dawn upon you, only as you "follow on to know the Lord."

Avoid for the present aught that would tend to dissipate your better feelings and more spiritual desires, and seek faithfully and earnestly, through communion and prayer, strength resolutely to choose the narrow path of life.

"When shall thy love constrain
  And draw me to thy breast?
When shall my soul return again
  To God, her only rest?

"Ah! what avails my strife,
  My wandering to and fro?
Thou giv'st the words of endless life:
  Ah! whither should I go?

"Here at thy feet I fall,
  I long to be made free;
I fain would now obey the call,
  And give up all for Thee."

LETTER V.

THE NEW BIRTH.

I FEAR that you are perplexing your mind with mere theological subtilties, and are hesitating in the plain path of duty, from a false expectation of what you think you ought to feel and experience. You know your inward needs; you are conscious that your past life has been sinful, that you have not cherished the true feelings of a child toward God, that, although surrounded by many religious influences, you have not hitherto regarded love to God and faith in Christ as the one thing needful; and you know too, that having been awakened, through the influences of the Spirit, to this sense of your spiritual wants, the religious choice, the yielding yourself up to these inward, divine promptings, lies wholly in your own power. No one can constrain you to make it, or can deter your from entering on, the only true path of life. It must be the resolve, the act, of your own free-will, resulting from an inward conviction of its fitness and its necessity, and of your obligation to your God and your Saviour.

But you are waiting to possess some peculiar feelings of interest in spiritual things, to realize some secret, entire change, something altogether different from anything hitherto experienced, before you think that you have any right to regard yourself as having truly entered upon the Christian course. The new birth seems to you something strange, and mysterious, something with which you have little to do,— a change to be wrought for you, not within you, and with your own co-operation.

Let us, then, understand distinctly what is implied in this phrase, what is its true meaning.

I reply, it is a change of aim, of purpose, of desire, of character; a change sometimes, indeed, effected suddenly to human sight,— the particular event or season of excitement to which it is ascribed being often the occasion rather than the cause of its development,— but generally a secret and gradual transformation of the inward life, begun on earth, to be completely consummated only in heaven. It is a change of motive and desire, the birth of the spiritual nature, the awakening of a spiritual conviction. With some, but with comparatively few in the present imperfect state of Christian society and education, this takes place very early in life. Where the child has been surrounded by religious influences, and has received a truly Christian education, his first thoughts, desires, and aspirations may be so directed heavenward, his earliest affections may be so fixed on the Redeemer, and through him he may so learn of the Father, that the world may never claim him for its own, nor chill the ardor of his young desires. The choice of the right, the true, the heavenly, may be his first conscious choice. But as in your case you have lived much of your past life unmindful of God, with slight personal interest in the truths revealed through Christ, with only transient emotions of gratitude, and with little reference to his will and example, so your life henceforth must be guided and regulated by reference not to self, but to God; not by mere worldly desires and aims, but by those laws of spiritual truth, duty, and obligation which are permanent and eternal.

And for all who have led for a longer or shorter period of time a mere worldly life, with little thought of eternal realities, and with little taste for religious pursuits and enjoyments,—with all in whom the merely earthly instincts and desires have triumphed over the spiritual, even for a little season,—there must be this inward awakening and renewal, this change of motives and aims, from the selfish and worldly to the spiritual, divine, and heavenly.

Such a change is rightly termed "being born again," so great, so important, so *essential* is it.

Without it, we cannot enter into the kingdom of heaven; we can know nothing of those spiritual desires, aims, affections, joys, that constitute the enjoyment, the blessedness, the peace, of that kingdom, — the kingdom that comes not with observation, but has its reign within, in the secret sanctuary of the soul.

It is a change wrought within by the Spirit of God, which never ceases to plead with us, and to bless us; our own hearts freely and consciously opening themselves to the reception of the Divine influence, and our whole souls going forth in the earnest prayer for an entire harmony of will and purpose with God; our lives attesting the sincerity of our aims, while we constantly look to the Spirit as our only sure source of strength and support.

To the eye of others, the routine of the outward life may often seem but little different after such renewal, after the new birth, after the deliberate, determined choice of the soul, especially where circumstances and education have so restrained and guarded the individual as to render flagrant acts of sin almost impossible, or when the native temperament has been of that serious, quiet cast which precludes sudden outbursts of temper and passion, and is often mistaken for true, religious goodness. But to the quickened, spiritual eye, that turns its glance inward in searching self-inspection, the world within, the life of the spirit, no longer seems as before. Old things are passing away, not at once, not suddenly, not without strenuous effort, watchfulness, and prayer, and the individual may not even be conscious of the exact time when this change, this new birth into the spiritual life, commences; nevertheless he is assured of its reality. He feels the inworking of new motives, of spiritual desires, of longings for a more perfect obedience, and a life more truly conformed to the spirit of Him whom he now acknowledges as the only Master of the soul. He is no longer satisfied with a correct moral life alone, with the regular performance of duties that seem fair and good to the world's eye, nor even with high and noble intellectual attainments: he has tested all of these, and found them wanting; for in all he has been serving self rather than God, forgetting that every power and faculty is but a stewardship from the Almighty Giver. But now he rejoices in a holier and higher light, and he knows its reality, not from mere feeling or emotion, but because he can trace within a more tender conscientiousness, a more faithful devotion to duty, a truer regard for the welfare of others, a warmer sympathy, a more enlarged charity. His prayers, too, are more sincere and fervent, and are no longer offered at stated times, from habit or a sense of duty, but because he esteems it his highest privilege to draw near his Father and his

Saviour in supplication and communion. His interest in direct religious duties is more heartfelt, and his sense of religious obligations more deep and abiding. He is conscious of a growing interest in spiritual truths, of cherished desires, aims, and purposes, which have no fulfilment in any worldly occupation or pleasure, but which ever point onward and upward for their full fruition. He is willing to walk in the solitary path of duty, or to choose such labors as may bring upon him obloquy and scorn from others, if he only feels that his Master calls him to the work; for fidelity to his Father and his Saviour has become the ruling desire and aim of his soul.

The common, every-day duties of life, and even the outward, material world, seem transfigured to his quickened spiritual vision.

> "With richer beauty glows
> The world, before so fair;
> Her holy light Religion throws,
> Reflected everywhere."

The changing seasons, — spring, with its bursting buds and promises of hope and beauty, and autumn, with its harvests of joy and hues of golden radiance; summer, in its rich luxuriance and fulness of life and gladness, and winter, with its icy breath and mantle of snow; day, with its light and life and ceaseless activity, and night, in its solemn stillness and blessed ministries of silence and repose, — all bring to his soul their own peculiar lessons of spiritual truth and blessing; for they whisper of

> "A Presence and a Spirit that impels
> All thinking objects, all objects of all thought,
> And rolls through all things."

Jonathan Edwards thus describes the same experience: "My sense of divine things gradually increased, and became more and more lively, and had more of inward sweetness. The appearance of everything was altered; there seemed to be, as it were, a calm, sweet cast or appearance of divine glory, in almost everything. God's excellency, his wisdom, his purity, and love, seemed to appear in the sun, moon, and stars; in the clouds and blue sky; in the grass, flowers, trees; in the water and all nature."

In fine, a radical and entire change — the introduction of new purposes, motives, and aims — is gradually taking place within his soul. In the language of Scripture, he is "born again," he is a new creature; not springing at once to the full stature of the mature Christian, not leaving at a single bound all old habits, wrong desires, selfish propensities, but, with the consciousness of having made the distinct and decided choice of Christ as the only Master of the soul, of obeying God and keeping his law, he goes on, day by day, conquering the evil, and, through the strength ever vouchsafed to the humble and sincere seeker, gaining new and higher attainments in the Christian life.

I have spoken of the new birth as being *generally* a silent and gradual change, a secret though certain transformation of the inward life. Yet the experience of faithful Christians, from the time of the Apostles to the present day, assures us that there are undoubted instances of conversion where the change is at once sudden and genuine; and do we not err in doubting the reality of such cases, and thus, in our secret thought, limiting the power of the Omnipotent? Can the soul turn from sin to God too soon or too suddenly? Do not our endeavors often lack earnestness, and our appeals fall lifeless upon the heart, because we have no true faith in the power of God to touch *at once* the secret springs of the soul? Do we not vainly limit the mighty influences of the Spirit to those earlier times when thousands were converted in a single day, and the Pentecostal song of gladness echoed from heart to heart its joyous notes of praise, — forgetting the still unchanging nature of God's attributes, the sacredness of his law, and his eternal promises through Christ, the same yesterday, to-day, and for ever?

At those moments when the Spirit of God moves over the soul, and searches its deepest and most hidden recesses, — when the brightness of his ineffable purity and holiness reveals the darkness and the evil within, — when the holiness of his law condemns the disobedience and sin of the alienated heart, and the depth of his love incarnated in the Saviour rebukes the secret ingratitude and melts the ice of the cold and selfish spirit, — then, convinced as never before of its inward want and destitution, acknowledging in grief and bitterness the worthlessness and sinfulness of the life unsanctified by the Father's presence and the Saviour's love, feeling the hatefulness of sin in the eye of perfect Holiness, and longing to be relieved from the burden of remorse, of an accusing conscience, and the sense of God's displeasure, it bows in agony and contrition at the foot of the cross, with the heartfelt confession of sin; and, at length, through the secret depths of the soul is heard that heavenly voice of pardon and of hope, " God so loved the world that he gave his only-begotten Son, that *whosoever* believeth in him should not perish, but have everlasting life." And with this blessed assurance, with faith in the reconciling love of God through Christ, with new aims and earnest prayers and longings for a spiritual life, the soul, though deeply conscious of sin and unworthiness, is yet " born again," and has " passed from death unto life," from being the mere creature of time and the slave of appetite and passion, to the living consciousness of being an immortal being, an heir of eternity, a child of God, redeemed through Christ, with the determined will and purpose of henceforth consecrating its whole powers and influence to the Master's service.

But whatever may have been your personal experience, examine anew, sincerely and prayerfully, your own heart. Test your motives, aims, and desires. Ask yourself such questions as these: What is now the ruling desire of my soul, what my prevailing aim? Am I seeking to live for what is pure, holy, and true, or am I absorbed in mere outward duties, in business, or dress, or fashion, or worldly frivolities? Do I feel a growing interest in religious truths and duties? Do I seek more constantly help from God, and does prayer seem no longer a mechanical form, but a blessed privilege? Have I a deeper sense of my own weakness, and a growing consciousness that my sufficiency is from God alone? Have I a truer faith in Christ, — a faith no longer of the intellect merely, but springing from my conscious heart-need of a Saviour and Redeemer? Am I becoming more conscientious, faithful, and diligent, more kind and charitable, more gentle and loving, more humble and self-denying? Am I gaining, day by day, more control over my passions and every wayward inclination? Am I growing more Christ-like in heart and in life?

Put such questions as these to yourself, simple yet comprehensive; and though unconscious perhaps of any sudden change, yet if you are able, as I trust, to answer them, in some good measure, in the affirmative, then may you feel, without any vain self-conceit, that you have indeed entered upon the true and narrow way, that the work of regeneration is truly and hopefully begun within your soul, and that God *will* work within you both to will and to do of his good pleasure.

"There are those of ripe experience, of high Christian attainments, of that heavenly-mindedness which is always serene and unclouded as the upper sky. But all this did not come of itself. Always when the internal experience of such persons is disclosed to us, we find that they reached those summits of peace through conflicts and watchings that sometimes chased repose from their pillows. The path of our regeneration is open and plain. It is simple self-denial until there is no self to be denied; and this is never accomplished without painful vigils and struggles and persevering toil, however smoothly our external affairs may flow on. . . . . . And yet we would not represent the Christian life as only a life of struggle. The region of eternal rest is not reached through a path of incessant upward toil. We go from one height to another, as hills rise above hills, and on every height gained we enjoy its partial peace. There are seasons when our wrong propensities are quiescent, and we rest from our labor until temptation wakes them up and the conflict begins anew. And when one of these enemies is destroyed, we have the peace of victory until another comes in sight, all the while rejoicing in our faith in Him who is our shield and buckler, and who gives us at these intervals the earnest of everlasting rest and progress."

While, then, you still cherish a deep sense of your own unworthiness and sin, of your past alienation from God, and of his violated law, remember also his words of promise through Christ, the forgiveness and the help vouchsafed to every penitent, seeking soul. "He that spared not his own Son, but delivered him up for us all, how shall he not with him also freely give us all things?" "Herein is love, not that we loved God, but that he loved us, and sent his Son to be the propitiation for our sins."

May He who has begun the good work within you, sustain and keep you, and nourish you in all spiritual truth and life, until you are wholly his.

LETTER VI.

CHRIST THE RECONCILER AND SAVIOUR.

YOU are conscious, my dear friend, of having made the distinct and heartfelt choice of the religious life. You are earnestly desirous of forming a truly Christian character, of leaving henceforth all your past indifference, coldness, and sin, all alienation from God, and backwardness in his service. You trust that you are sincerely penitent for the past, and you long for a higher, truer, nobler life, than you have hitherto led,—for a full, entire consecration of yourself to God. But you say that you are still restless and dissatisfied; that you are not conscious of any definite, constant progress; that sin still gains the mastery, and old habits of thought and feeling cling to you with a tenacious grasp. While you acknowledge in the secrecy of your soul the supremacy of the unseen and spiritual, such motives have not that control over your daily life which you believe they ought to possess in the Christian heart, and you cannot feel assured of the forgiveness and acceptance of God.

Allow me, then, to point out to you some causes which have led to your present state of feeling, and to direct you to the only true path of peace.

While your penitence has been sincere, your choice true and deliberate, your steps turned to the one narrow and rugged path of life, there still lurks in your soul a secret feeling, that in some way what you have thus far accomplished merits the approval of Heåven, — that your own righteousness will be sufficient, as it were, to open the celestial gates of peace and to insure the word of pardon.

There is, with all your consciousness of sin and imperfection, a concealed, and yet a baneful sense of self-sufficiency in your soul,—a pride of purpose, — a feeling that you can accomplish something as of yourself, and so approve yourself, which is nothing but self-righteousness. Like Christian, you have turned aside from the sure, though narrow path, and, quitting your faithful guide, have vainly sought help of Mr. Legality, and have found, like him, your burden only becoming the heavier and more difficult to bear.

The voice of conscience has spoken loudly and clearly within your soul, and has not been unheeded; but you have yet to learn that conscience, without a reconciling Christ, lacks peace as well as strength; for, as another has well said, "the mere moral or conscience system of life excludes the most powerful principle of disinterested action, which is a grateful love and trust in a personal help, flowing infinitely from God, through Christ and his cross. Then, too, it engenders the poor habit of continual self-reference, self-measurement, and self-centralization, instead of taking the soul up above itself, giving it an object there to live for in faith and love. It sets consciousness above revelation, as a light to the mysteries of our inner life; and that consciousness is a dim candle over a deep mine."

Strive as you will, you will never fulfil the perfect law of God, that which demands that every thought even shall be brought into captivity and entire obedience. Where then do you stand? Merit is out of the question. Self-exaltation is abashed. Pride is rebuked. "The aspiration after the perfect in all noble natures is the mightiest hunger of the heart. But if no blessed promise of forgiveness is to come by faith, and comfort its failures, all its yearnings are tortures, and it is only the mightiest tormenter of the heart."

Is there no peace, then, for the restless, penitent, aspiring soul? Is life to be passed in this constant struggle, this inward uneasiness, this consciousness of the imperfection of the work, compared with the purity and holiness of the requirement? Is there to be constant dissatisfaction and restlessness and self-upbraiding, with no clear beacon-light of hope and trust to brighten the narrow path, and guide the trembling steps?

Let the blessed words of the Redeemer answer your anxious self-questionings. "Come unto me, and I will give you rest. I am the light of the world; he that followeth me shall not walk in darkness, but shall have the light of life. This is the new covenant in my blood, shed for many, for the *remission of sins*." And again, hear the Apostle's joyful declaration: "Now, in Christ Jesus, ye who sometime were afar off, are made nigh by the blood of Christ. God commendeth his love toward us, in that while we were *yet sinners*, Christ died for us. For if, when we were enemies, we were reconciled to God by the death of his Son, much more, being reconciled, we shall be saved by his life. Therefore, being justified by faith, we have peace with God through our Lord Jesus Christ. In whom we have redemption through his blood, even the forgiveness of our sins." And as if these assurances were not sufficient, we have the words of the beloved disciple: "God so loved the world, that he gave his only-begotten Son, that whosoever believeth in him should not perish, but have everlasting life. If *any man* sin, we have an advocate with the Father, Jesus Christ the righteous; and he is the propitiation for our sins, and not for ours only, but also for the sins of the whole world." Here, then, is your true answer: "By grace are ye saved, through faith, not of works, lest any man should boast";—not because you have attained, either are already perfect, but because of the supreme desire, the ruling love, the trusting faith of the soul, casting aside all self-confidence, and resting its only hope on the free promises of God, through Christ, the reconciler and intercessor.

Look, then, away from yourself to Christ. Turn your eyes from this anxious self-inspection to the cross on Calvary. Hear those divine words, "Look unto me, and be ye saved, all the ends of the earth." See the fulness, the depth of the love there revealed; and while the contemplation of that divine sacrifice, thus needed to move and melt your soul, thus needed for your personal reconciliation, pardon, and acceptance, discloses to you as nothing else can your own inward evil and sin, the heights of God's perfect holiness, and the depths of his divine compassion,—while it leads you to exclaim with the prodigal's penitence, "Father, I have sinned against heaven and before thee,"—let it also speak of pardon and strength and hope. Doubt not the promises of the Almighty, through his holy Son, thus tenderly interceding with man. If, in sincerity, we confess and lament, and seek to turn from our sins, "He is *faithful* and *just* to forgive us our sins." Mark these words. He not only promises forgiveness, but the promise is in full accordance with his faithfulness and justice, as manifested in the cross of Christ, — in perfect harmony with his free, divine, and ceaseless love, — quickening the soul too, by that joyous hope, that, through his Spirit and his Son, He will at length "cleanse us from all unrighteousness."

There is a state of mind, not founded on true humility, which questions the reality of its own penitence and the forgiveness of God, from a lurking, half-acknowledged feeling — seldom actually expressed in words, or even distinctly brought before the inward vision, until some sudden revelation of God's providence draws aside the thin veil of self-deception — that God is unable thus to forgive, thus to justify the soul through Christ. It questions the Divine omnipotence, not so much from any distinct purpose of so doing, as because it secretly, but falsely imagines, that by cherishing such feelings it deepens its own poor humility; forgetting meanwhile that such doubting of the promises of God is, in itself, an actual and presumptuous sin.

Cast aside, then, once for all, your idle self-questionings; cast aside your weary strivings for reconciliation and peace, without Christ and his cross; cast aside your vain scepticism as to God's own promises. What more could he have done for you than he has done? While he embodies his divine love and compassion in that Holy One cradled in the manger at Bethlehem, manifests through him his own infinite purity and tenderness, incarnating the depths of his love and his perfect holiness in that Lord of suffering, mingles there that mightiest expression of his abhorrence of all sin, and of his yearning love over the sinner, — why should you turn away, as if this were a sort of world's exhibition, having no peculiar voice of awakening or assurance to *your* soul?

Arise from your doubts and misgivings. Cast away your tattered, unseemly garment of self-righteousness, and come joyfully into the life of reconciliation, and of a humble Christian hope. It is no human voice that whispers in your soul's better moments, "I have visited thee; I have redeemed thee; thou art mine." Trust the promises of God through Christ; — not in a vain spirit of *meriting* aught of the Divine favor, but because you are conscious of the desire and purpose of consecrating yourself wholly to him, of being moved, swayed, governed by his will. Leave, henceforth, all your past alienation, all your doubts of the Divine promises, and hear those blessed words, "Come out from among them, and be ye separate, saith the Lord, and I will be a Father to you, and ye shall be my sons and daughters, saith the Lord Almighty."

Even so I have known one for years struggling with the darkness of an unsatisfied faith, desiring sincerely to be a true Christian in heart and life, yet longing in vain for any definite assurance or cheerful hope, until in God's holy providence the veil of self-deception was removed, the thought of meriting the Divine approval was cast for ever aside, the sin of doubting his word of promise through Christ was clearly seen, and from that reconciling cross of suffering was heard the blessed word of pardon; and as a sweet benediction fell upon the weary soul the heavenly response, "I will be to *thee* a Father; and thou shalt be my child."

Dwell often in secret and prayerful contemplation upon this sublime theme, — of the reconciling love of God, manifested in the life and teachings, the sufferings and the cross, of the Redeemer. Let your daily, fervent prayer be, —

"Lead me, O Spirit, to the Son,
To feel and know what he has done;
To lay me low before the cross,
And reckon all beside as dross;
To speak, and think, and act, and move,
And love, as thou wouldst have me love."

Go, in your conscious weakness and sin, in your doubts and misgivings, and devoutly thank God that he has led you to feel your dependence upon Christ as a personal Saviour.

"Let not conscience make you linger,
Nor of fitness idly dream;

All the fitness he requireth,
Is to feel your *need* of him."

Draw nigh, then, unto God, in full assurance of faith, through his own appointed Mediator; draw nigh in the simple, confiding trust and confidence of a child; and then will he, pouring out upon you the spirit of adoption, make you feel the reconciliation, the joy, the peace, of one of his children. And through whatever secret discipline God may appoint, may you at length be enabled, trustingly, to exclaim, "I know that my Redeemer liveth, and am persuaded that he is able to keep that which I have committed unto him!" This living faith may not come at once; you may have long to seek, and press, and strive; but "though it tarry, wait for it; because it will surely come: it will not tarry." "He that cometh to me shall never hunger, and he that believeth on me shall never thirst."

"What blessed effects does the love of God produce in the hearts of those who abide in him!" writes Lady Huntington to Charles Wesley. "How solid is the peace, and how divine the joy, that springs from an assurance that we are united to the Saviour by a living faith! Blessed be his name. I have an abiding sense of his presence with me, notwithstanding the weakness and unworthiness I feel. After the poor labors of the day are over, my heart still cries, 'God be merciful to me a sinner!' But I can ever add, 'Thanks be unto him for a Saviour and Redeemer.'" — May such a faith and peace be yours, through Christ the Reconciler and Intercessor!

LETTER VII.

CHRIST THE SANCTIFIER.

The last letter addressed to you would be incomplete and unsatisfying, did I not point you to Christ as the Sanctifier, no less than as the Reconciler of the soul unto God,—as him through whom alone you have the full promise and assurance of forgiveness, and the hope of the Divine acceptance. Some persons seem vainly to imagine that salvation is something wholly external to them, something existing in the far-off future alone, forgetting that the only true kingdom of heaven is within, having its commencement even now and here, and that the highest degree of outward happiness and success would be wholly unsatisfying and incomplete, without the inward spirit of faith and love and trust;—that the great redemption which Christ has brought to us lies in freedom from the power of sin itself, in meeting that deep, *present* need of the soul, of which I have already spoken. And herein we perceive the perfect harmony of the separate yet united offices he bears to the individual spirit.

The blessed assurance, "Thy sins are forgiven thee," breathes over the soul its holy benediction of peace, only to gird it anew for daily conflict with evil and temptation, and to whisper in its gentle accents of love and entreaty, "Go and sin no more."

Comparatively easy would it be to maintain the fervor of our desires, the loftiness of our aims, the spirituality of our aspirations, were our watchfulness requisite only in the hours of solitude and retirement; did the secrecy of the closet, or the quiet watches of the night, alone witness our struggles with sin and wrong desire and evil passion. But to carry our convictions of truth and of duty into the conflicts of daily life, to evince a quiet fortitude, a Christian spirit of love, forbearance, and forgiveness, under petty provocations, to quench the rising passion and speak the gentle word, to maintain an unblemished integrity, to be consistent under every circumstance with our acknowledged aims, to assert in every scene and season, by a pure and blameless and spiritual walk among men, the supremacy of the unseen and spiritual, — here lies the true arena of our conflict, here the broad theatre where we are to prove the truth of our Christian convictions and purposes.

Here, too, you have often felt wearied and disheartened. Conscious of so much in your heart and life inconsistent with the commands of God and the perfect example of Christ, — seeing the heights of Christian attainment towering ever higher and higher above you, — you have sometimes yielded to the sense of your own utter weakness and short-coming, and have felt that the conflict was too great for you, that your life would never express your true aims and loftier purposes. Yet just here lies the hardest conflict, with all noble, aspiring natures. This higher aspiration, this longing for a nobler life, for a more rapid and consistent progress, compared with the imperfection and insufficiency of the actual attainment, is no unreal or mere fanciful struggle. Unless met and sustained by a Christian faith and hope, it presses upon the soul with a crushing and deadening sense of utter insufficiency and personal weakness. Faith grows dim, resistance flags, the star of hope is dimmed, and the soul either sinks into a dreary darkness or a lethargic sleep of indifference.

But at this very point, when the light of the Spirit has revealed to you the weakness, the imperfection, the sin within, — when you shrink from the life-long conflict, and fear for your own progress and perseverance in the true path, — at this very point Christ again meets you with his blessed words of encouragement and hope, promising to do that, in and for you, which you cannot do of yourself. He came not alone through his death to proclaim assurance of pardon, and to seal the promise of acceptance; but through his life, through his teachings, through his fervent intercessions, and, more than all, through his ever-present spirit as the Comforter, the Sanctifier of the soul, to renew it in the Divine image, to quicken it to newness of life, to breathe into it a divine strength, to sustain it in conflict, to live within it, as its only true life.

"Abide in me, and I in you." Have you ever fathomed the deep meaning of this promise in your hours of regret, dissatisfaction, or discouragement? You are not laboring and striving alone. A mightier and holier than man is with you, nearer to you than the truest of earthly friends, and if you will but listen and yield yourself unreservedly to his guidance, his word of encouragement ever is, "My strength shall be made perfect in thy weakness"; "I *will* give to him who is athirst, of the fountain of the water of life freely." "I am the Bread of Life. He that cometh to me shall never hunger, and he who believeth on me shall never thirst." "Lo, I am with you alway!" Do we ask more? "If ye, being evil, know how to give good gifts unto your children, how much more shall your Father in heaven give the *Holy Spirit* to them that ask him." "Peace I leave with you, *my* peace I give unto you. Let not your heart be troubled, neither let it be afraid."

And again, in the assured language of the

Apostle, — an epitome of the whole Gospel revelation of pardon and reconciliation and renewal, — "After that the kindness and love of God toward man appeared, not by works of righteousness which we have done, but according to his mercy, he saved us, by the washing of regeneration and renewing of the Holy Ghost, which he shed on us abundantly, through Jesus Christ our Saviour." Through Christ abiding with you, with the sustaining influences of his grace and the quickening power of his Spirit, go forth then, firmly yet humbly, to meet the daily conflict within and around you, in the spirit and faith of Paul resolutely exclaiming, "I can of mine own self do nothing, but through Christ strengthening me I can do all things."

"Maintain only an unchangeable resolution of obedience, and an upright intention towards God, and all will be well. Christ sent forth his early disciples, not to luxury, but to conflict; not to honor, but to contempt; not to amusement, but to labor; not to take repose, but to bring forth much fruit with patience." Even so he sends forth every true-hearted follower to grow strong through endurance, and resolute by stringent exertion; animating them by his own example, quickening them by his felt presence, sanctifying, purifying, and redeeming them by his own indwelling, co-working Spirit.

Go not forth, then, to your daily duties, and

joys, and conflicts, as if alone. Go not forth from the secrecy of your closet, as if you left there all peace and heavenly companionship; but go as in the Master's presence; go strengthened with might from his spirit in the inner man; go in the spirit of that noble artist of old,

> "Who never moved his hand
> Till he had steeped his inmost soul in prayer";

go in trust, and faith, and cheerful hope; and so may strength from the Most High quicken your often feeble endeavors and distrusting heart, and may Christ ever abide with you, and the Spirit sanctify you wholly!

LETTER VIII.

PERSONAL ACCEPTANCE.

In your last letter you ask, "How shall I truly know that I am personally the subject of this sanctifying influence? Is there not presumption, a sort of self-conscious pride, in saying, with any degree of certainty or assurance, that I indeed belong to Christ, that I possess such a measure of faith and holiness as to be called a child of God?" I reply, None of us can be *absolutely* certain of a future salvation, because so long as we live we are in danger of falling; but we can know the present state of our souls in relation to God and to Christ; we can be sure that we are *seeking* an inward renewal, that our aims, purposes, desires, are heavenward and spiritual. In the words of another: "We can be sure that we are *on the right way;* not sure that we love God with all our heart, but sure that we do love him sincerely and really; not sure that we are obedient in all things, but sure that it is our aim and purpose to obey; not sure that our faith and penitence are what they should be, but that we have the germs of true penitence and the seeds of a right faith. We may know that we have passed from death unto life,—know that, whereas we were once blind, now we see,—know that we are sincere in our purpose and our effort, and that we have a peace and a joy within, from communing with God, which cannot be taken from us. . . . . . We need to *feel* that our sins are forgiven, and that we are the children of God. With such a conviction clear and strong in our hearts, duty is pleasure, trial is happiness. Without it, how hard to struggle against sin! how hard to make daily resolutions, strive with daily temptations, begin continually an ever-recurring warfare!"

Now, such an assurance can be ours only through prayer, self-examination, a personal application of the words of Scripture, and a faithful listening to the voice of the Spirit within, which must either acquit or condemn us; for it is "the Spirit that beareth witness with our spirits that we are the children of God." And "the fruit of the Spirit is love, joy, peace, long-suffering, gentleness, goodness, faith, patience." Of course, these fruits are not seen in their ripeness and maturity at once, but you can judge whether they are the growing traits of your character, whether the soul is gradually yet surely conforming itself to the Master's image, whether it is your sincere and daily prayer that such may be yours.

Then you have many other test-proofs, scattered throughout the whole New Testament. "To such as believe, Christ is precious. Truly our fellowship is with the Father, and with his Son, Jesus Christ. Hereby know we that we dwell in him, and he in us, because he hath given us of his Spirit. He that believeth on the Son of God hath the witness in himself. The love of God is shed abroad in our hearts, through the Holy Spirit. Whoso keepeth his word, in him verily is the love of God perfected."

While your only standard of self-judgment is that of your Divine Master, let me again entreat you not to perplex and distress yourself because your present life displays not fully the *ripened* fruits of the mature Christian. Only be sure that your penitence has been sincere, your consecration full and entire, your self-confidence displaced by a firm, entire reliance on the promises of God, that, through the Spirit, he will work in and with you to will and to do of his good pleasure, — then doubt not his power to sanctify you *wholly*, and, through Christ, to redeem you from the inward power of sin. Trust in the Divine help. Trust faithful efforts of duty. Trust in the assured answer to all sincere prayer. We rob ourselves of our true peace, and so of all earnestness and effective endeavors, when we thus doubt the simple promises of God. "We linger too much in the old Jewish notion of being saved by the works of the Law. There is a sense in which Christ is our Redeemer, which many of us have hardly yet begun to fathom. We need to draw nearer to Him, to think less of our own deeds, and more of what he has done and promised, and is even now doing for us. We need to feel that, after all short-comings and failures, there is still acceptance of the soul with God, through what Christ has revealed, through faith in him as the manifestation of the Father, assuring us of forgiveness and remission of sins, simply because our hearts are given to him. The penitence, the aim, the self-consecration, the faith, — this is it, that renders a soul acceptable to God and to Christ, not because it is spotless or sinless." Realizing this, while we watch and pray, and strive against sin, and fear to grieve away the Spirit, shall we not rest more confidingly in the condescending grace and all-surpassing goodness of God?

But here you ask, "How shall I know that I truly love God and Christ? How be assured that the conditions of acceptance are fulfilled?"

Let the revealed word again make answer. "This is the love of God, that we keep his commandments. He that hath my commandments and keepeth them, he it is that loveth me."

True love is to be judged of by its fruits, rather than by the mere feeling or emotion it excites, at the passing moment, towards any particular object of affection, — its fruits of loyalty, obedience, cheerful self-sacrifice, self-denying exertion, patience, forbearance, fidelity.

This is the true and better part of affection, manifesting itself in the daily life and conversation; and without this the mere emotional feeling, however apparently strong and ardent, would be utterly futile and worthless. The ardor and intensity of such feelings depend in a great measure upon the natural constitution and temperament of the individual; and we have no right to judge of the state of one's religious affections merely by the warmth of his zeal, or the fervor of his expressions of interest.

Emotion has well been termed the "tidal wave" of affection, ebbing and flowing with the current of passing circumstances; "but in the deep, full reservoir, sheltered from the wind, there can be no wave. Emotion makes us conscious of affection, as the waves do of our motion upon the water, though affection may be as deep without emotion as with it, as the ocean is no less deep in calm than in storm. Nay, shallow affection may be liable to the most agitating emotions, as the most shallow of our great lakes is heaved by a quick, short swell, such as never stirs the profounder bosom of the deep." The deeper affection, the obedience, the love, the trust, which abides unmoved amid every change and fluctuation and restless beating of the outward life, which only believes the more confidently and trusts the more implicitly when the darkness gathers and trials encompass the path, which obeys without questioning and acts without hesitation at the call of duty, however arduous or difficult, — this is the true love of the Christian heart, this the standard of self-judgment. "Wherefore by their *fruits* ye shall know them. Not every one who saith, Lord, Lord, shall enter into the kingdom of heaven, but he who *doeth* the will of my Father in heaven." And in the last interview of our Saviour with Peter, the most impulsive, ardent, and enthusiastic of all the little band of Apostles, how strikingly does he guard him against any reliance on mere feeling, or momentary glow of emotion, when, after thrice drawing from him the confession of his deep attachment to the Master, whom he had as often denied, he leaves him with the emphatic command, — as if its fulfilment were the only true pledge of his real affection and devotedness to his service, — "Feed my sheep, feed my lambs!"

But while you seek, in your seasons of self-examination, this only reliable proof of love to God and to Christ, do not believe that all warmth, fervor, and glow of feeling are wholly out of your power. The affections, no less than the powers of thought and intellect, grow stronger and deeper in proportion to their true exercise.

The laws of action and of reaction are equal. It is a remark ascribed to St. Augustine, that "prayer is the measure of love," which implies that those who love much will pray much, and, conversely, that those who pray much will love much.

We cannot, it is true, love a mere abstraction, an impalpable something, simply because we believe we *ought* so to love. Truly to love God we must know him, — know him as our Father, as our best, truest, nearest Friend; feel him near to us in every bright and joyous, and in every clouded and trying, scene of life; speaking to us in the glad sunshine and the darkened cloud, — in the dewy freshness of the summer morn, and the calm and glowing radiance of the sunset hour, — in the gorgeous tints of the autumn forests, and the opening leaves and bursting buds of the joyous spring; drawing near to us in all our daily walks; encompassing our path and our lying down; spreading around us the comforts, the blessings, of each passing day; filling our tables with plenty; sending the pulses of health bounding through our veins; blessing us in countless forms and ways, or withholding such gifts of his bounty only the more truly to draw our hearts to Him, only to crown us with a yet more enduring loving-kindness and a yet more tender mercy.

But, above all, to love God we must know

him as manifested in Christ, — know him as incarnated in human form, — know him as revealing his holiness, his tenderness, his pity, his forbearance, his yearning love and condescending grace, in the suffering, glorified Redeemer. Here you *can* fix your full and earnest regard. Here, through a growing sense of your own inward wants and failings, you can enter into personal companionship with a strength made perfect in weakness. Here you can sit at the very feet of One who knows you wholly, who has been tried through sorrow and desertion and all forms of human suffering, and who can and does feel with you and for you in every secret struggle and every spiritual aspiration. Here is no vain abstraction, but the Father thus condescendingly manifesting himself to his children, as if to awaken in them those deep, fervent emotions of love and of trust which form the only true, living, and enduring bond between the Parent and the child.

Study, then, the life and character of Christ, until he stands before you in his spiritual power and divine glory, — until in your inmost soul you feel that he alone meets those secret cravings and wants which point you to him as your Saviour and Redeemer. And by such contemplation, by prayer and spiritual communion, love will grow in your soul, — the feeling, the affection, the emotion of love, as well as a more confirmed obedience, a more stringent loyalty, a more faithful adherence to duty.

But let me entreat you not to be disheartened, as some are, because this deeper emotion is often wanting, or because your feelings seldom reach the level of your aspirations. The noble refrain of Paul, "I am persuaded that neither life nor death, nor angels nor principalities nor powers, nor things present, nor things to come, nor height nor depth, nor any other creature, can separate us from the love of God that is in Christ Jesus our Lord," was the result of years of conflict, faith, and prayer; the faith kindling the love, and the love ever reacting, and quickening and strengthening the faith and the obedience. As has been well said: "The want of such emotional feelings may sometimes be regarded as a misfortune; but it should not discourage the Christian who persists in his obedience. The truth is, that obedience in this situation, as being more difficult, may be considered as more disinterested, and pure, and acceptable to God." If your emotions are dull and sluggish upon other themes, you have no reason to expect intense fervor and glow when you contemplate those of the highest and most spiritual character. Only be sure that your aims and purposes are true and heavenly, that your ruling desire is for the life hid with Christ in God, that your daily striving is for a closer conformity to the spirit of your

Master, and obedience to his commands. Then distress not yourself because you do not always *feel* just as you wish and desire, because your affections are not so quick nor your love so fervent as you would fain experience. God reads your inmost heart. He sees the secret purpose and the inward longing, — the longing to know him more fully, to love him more fervently, to believe on him more trustingly, as he has manifested himself in the Redeemer. And the soul thus turned to him he will not leave to itself, to vain efforts at self-excitation. He *will* impart what you need; he will quicken and animate, strengthen and sustain. He who spared not his own Son, shall he not give, in his own time, all those feelings of love you desire, all those deeper emotions of gratitude, and confiding trust in his all-embracing goodness and loving-kindness, which you earnestly long for?

Only be faithful to the means offered to you, — faithful to those means of inward quickening which God has placed within your own control, — faithful in prayer, communion, and the earnest study of the revealed word, — faithful in watchfulness and self-examination, — faithful in tracing the Father's hand in all the trivial events of each passing day, — faithful in looking unto Jesus; then doubt not the assured promise, "He that seeketh, findeth; and to him that knocketh, it shall be opened."

Remember too the comforting thought of an old English poet in such moments of self-questioning, coldness, and doubt, "that our Heavenly Father does in truth take the will for all in all."

> "And when the heart says, (sighing to be approved,)
> 'O could I love!' and stops, God writeth 'Loved'!"

I have thus endeavored to point out to you some of the plain and simple tests by which you may judge of your true spiritual state, and of your right to accept the clear, full promises of God. Not at once, I repeat, not by any one earnest resolve or stringent effort, can you attain the stature of the perfect Christian; but

> "Day by day with strength supplied,
> Through the life of Him who died,"

go forth, in trusting faith, to the combat with sin and evil within and around you, remembering the quickening words of the beloved disciple: "It doth not yet appear what we shall be; but we know that, when he shall appear, we shall be like him, for we shall see him as he is; and every man that hath this hope in him purifieth himself, even as he is pure." And again he says: "These things have I written unto you that believe on the name of the Son of God, that ye may *know* that ye have eternal life, and that ye may believe on the name of the Son of God. And this is the confidence that we have in him, that, if we ask anything according to his will, he heareth us; and if we know that he hears us, whatsoever we ask, we know that we have the petitions that we desired of him."

May this purer love, and warmer devotion, and deeper assurance of faith, be yours, in God's own time and way!

LETTER IX.

THE TRUE SPHERE OF LIFE.

FROM your last letter, my dear friend, I fear that you are in danger of becoming dissatisfied with your present circle of duties, and the comparatively retired sphere of life in which Providence has placed you, and are cherishing a secret feeling, that in some more commanding position, in some wider and more conspicuous field, you could accomplish more fully the great ends of existence, could exert a larger influence, and do more for the cause of Christ and the promotion of his truth in the world. Now I will not reprove you for this feeling, for it is far from being a strange or unnatural one. There is an almost universal tendency in the human mind to aspire and seek after objects above and beyond its immediate sphere of operations, accompanied at the same time by more or less discontent with present pursuits, duties, and occupations. Sometimes it expresses itself in an undefinable restlessness, or a peevish discontent, and again in a morbid sensitiveness, or an impatient longing for something more definite, complete, and satisfying. It looks not at the sphere immediately around it, but imagines that in the distant future there must exist some situation, some position of influence, of duty, and effort, more in consonance with its individual capacities and powers. The feeling is confined to no age or condition, to no particular class in society and no special routine of daily duty. It is the natural expression of all aspiring souls, and when placed under the control of *religious principle*, and converted into a *holy* ambition, forms one of the chief motive powers to effort, progress, and advancement; otherwise it is a constant source of unhappiness, discontent, and weariness.

If the Master would only bid us do some great thing, something to excite attention and admiration, something that would lead even to the burning stake or the cross of shame, how gladly would we press forward to the conflict! But to go on, day after day, patiently seeking the conquest over inward passion and sin, performing "the trivial round and common task" of daily duty, — this is too monotonous, too humbling. Pride shrinks away abashed, and a thirst for human admiration steals imperceptibly into the soul, too often withering all its higher aims and holier aspirations.

But you ask, How shall I indeed know that I

am filling my true sphere of life, — that assigned me by Divine Providence?

I reply, God places us in such situations in life, and opens to us such spheres of duty, as are best suited to our individual capacities, talents, and spiritual needs; and when new duties and new spheres are assigned to us, to the prayerful, watchful, and self-forgetting spirit, there are always clear and definite indications by which to judge of the true path, by which to distinguish the leadings of Providence from a mere restless love of change, or discontent with the simple routine of daily duty.

In the performance of the humbler duties of life, in quiet home circles or on the arena of daily toil and business, most of us are called to fight the good warfare, and prove ourselves true Christians. Comparatively few are called to be an Oberlin or a Howard, a Judson or a Boardman, a Catherine Adorna or an Elizabeth Fry; for noble as are such exhibitions of the Christian spirit, — nay, I would rather say, such exemplifications of the divine life in the human soul, — they rather stand before us as beacon-lights to show the power of self-sacrifice and self-renunciation imparted to every Christian heart, if only the consecration be unreserved and entire; to manifest the living spirit which can alone impart vitality and power to any sphere of life, whether narrow or extended to the world's eye.

And by what inherent right do we call any sphere circumscribed or limited?

Spiritual power is not confined to narrow walls or small apartments, to the nursery or school-room, to the couch of weary pain and languishing, to the workshop or the ledger. It needs no trumpet to herald its authority, no banner of fashion to reveal its potent sway, no applause of the multitude to proclaim its true greatness and authority. Silently and secretly it achieves its true victories in the quiet sanctuary of home, by humble firesides and cottage hearths, in the abodes of poverty as well as in the circles of luxury, by the bed of lingering illness and chronic infirmity, in devotion to helpless infancy and feeble age, in the instruction of the ignorant, patience towards the wayward, fidelity to uncongenial duties, forbearance and gentleness, love and charity. Its utterances, though simple and unpretending, are fraught with intense power; for how often the slightest word uttered in true sincerity, and falling on the prepared spirit, has an efficacy in inspiring a living and vital faith, which no direct effort, no attempt at influence, could ever exert!

Christ does not call upon all of us to be apostles or martyrs, preachers or missionaries. When one whom he had healed sought to express his devotion and love by following him with his disciples, he bade him rather go home to his friends, and make known in that narrower circle what great things the Lord had done for him. And so he bids most of us take up his cross and bear it faithfully and resolutely in our own households, to proclaim the worth and the authority of a living faith, by an uncompromising integrity, a rigid fidelity, a tender regard, a gentle compassion, a forbearing love, and a Christ-like walk and conversation.

I have known one for years confined to his couch, by a most painful, chronic infirmity, cut off in opening manhood from every bright prospect which talent and education opened before him; for months and years unable to move a limb without the greatest suffering, even the light of heaven shut out at times from his secluded apartment, and hardly able to bear even the gentlest touch of a mother's or a sister's hand; and yet from that chamber of suffering and weariness and seclusion, there went forth, through his triumphant spirit of faith, and cheerful trust, and Christian self-forgetfulness, an influence to sustain, to quicken, and to animate,—a pure and holy influence, which only His eye that looks through the immortal ages can ever measure.

I have known, too, the gentle and devoted sister and daughter, seldom spoken of in the circles of fashion or mere gayety, never seeking to bring herself into notice, but evincing her cheerful, trusting, self-forgetting spirit in the quietness of home, pouring forth her rich treasures of love, and faithfully cultivating her powers of mind and heart, the better to contribute to the happiness of the little circle which her gentleness and thoughtfulness retained under her influence; and though early and suddenly called away to higher spheres of duty and usefulness, yet through her Christ-like spirit and holy trust leaving in the hearts of all who knew and loved her a sense of the reality of the Christian faith and hope, whose quickening and animating power eternity alone can reveal.

I have known, too, the abodes of poverty and desolation made rich by a heavenly faith and trust; suffering sanctified by prayer and patience; love and tenderness softening the sterner aspects of unremitting toil and care; self-denial and patience and holy faith writing their ineffaceable signet on brows consecrated by the baptism of trial and sorrow; and amid such scenes of earthly want and care, amid scenes, often repulsive to the mere worldly eye of fashion, again and again have I felt, how often in the sight of Heaven the standard of mere human judgment is reversed, and in a true Christian influence and power the last become first, and the first last.

Have you considered such truths, however, and do you still feel dissatisfied and uncertain with regard to your true sphere of life and duty? I reply, By a close and strict self-examination, without flattery or self-deception, learn whether your powers, your attainments, your endeavors, are such as would fit you for a wider sphere, or a more commanding position than you now occupy. Then ask yourself, if *now* you are faithfully filling your present sphere, if you are making *that* sphere as large as it is your duty to make it, and whether in your present position you are earnestly and perseveringly seeking the development of your highest moral and intellectual powers.

Look at the circumstances in which Providence has placed you, and see if there are not, in these, indications of your true sphere, — if there are not duties immediately around you which constitute the first and highest claim upon you.

> "Not by deeds that win the crowd's applauses,
> Not by works that give thee world-renown,
> Not by martyrdom, or vaunted crosses,
> Canst thou win and wear the *immortal* crown.
>
> "Daily struggling, though oft tried and lonely,
> Every day a rich reward will give;
> Thou wilt find, by hearty striving only,
> And truly loving, thou canst truly live."

If such be not the case, if you feel that, as you are now situated, your powers are cramped, your higher energies repressed, your nobler faculties undeveloped, if the promptings of the Spirit point you to other duties and new pursuits, then have you a right to seek a different sphere, and in a wider and more commanding circle to endeavor to accomplish the highest purposes of life.

But do you still feel these higher aspirations, these longings for wider circles of influence; and are you conscious, at the same time, that there are circumstances which forbid your seeking a different sphere, so that it would be a manifest violation of duty to desert your present position? Then feel assured, that these very circumstances are in reality the best for you, the true means through which you are to develop your highest spiritual powers.

Seek to be conscientious and faithful *where you are.* Watch for daily opportunities of growth and progress; and if, at times, you feel that some of your powers have not their full scope, remember that the blessing of God ever rests on the consecrated and childlike spirit. Remember also, that this is but the commencement of life, and if you are but true to yourself, use will be found for the powers here faithfully cultivated, in the holier exercises, the higher duties, and the larger sphere of the future life.

God has best resources; he makes flowers bloom, and waterfalls dash, and innumerable signs of beauty reveal themselves, where no eye sees them, where no foot of man ever trod Be content, then, earnestly to press on, and to let some of your powers grow and ripen in silence. Feel that you are but an instrument in the hand of God, and that if, now, to some are committed larger and wider ministries of influence, hereafter we are to be judged according to our opportunities and talents alone.

In the words of another, "You must not say, that in your sphere you can do little or nothing. Be patient, be confiding; you do not choose your sphere. Prepare yourself for greater usefulness by fidelity in the path Providence now marks out for you; avail yourself of opportunities to bear witness to the truth, as far as these are given. Cultivate in yourself the disinterested, mild, generous, resolute spirit of Jesus Christ. In these ways accumulate moral power, and be assured that openings for its exercise will multiply. Nothing helps us to discover means of doing good, like growing better and stronger. Be grateful that in any way, or to any degree, you may be God's minister on earth."

Had we but a child-like faith, and a simple confidence in God, we should no longer be perplexed by such anxious questionings and restless strivings. Too much do we feel as if the world depended upon our feeble efforts, and not on the Divine Providence. Too prone are we to forget that we are but instruments in His hands, and that all efforts are in vain, unless made under the guidance and blessing of the Divine spirit. Let there be action indeed, earnest, faithful, devoted action, but let this be preceded by an entire self-surrender, by a willingness to yield all with a simple trust to the Father, to follow Christ wherever he may lead.

As this living faith and trust become a more vital reality to your soul, so will the peace of God more truly dwell within it. The doubts that arise with regard to the sphere of life and the fit path of duty will gradually be dispersed, and a clearer and fuller light will shine upon your way.

Remember also, that the quiet and secret influence of Christian faith is greater than the widest array of philanthropic effort. This can be cultivated in every sphere, and under every circumstance of life, and it implies no strange, unnatural, or complex state of mind. It is simply a childlike trust in the Father, and a ready obedience to the Master, the life daily and hourly answering the question, "Lord, what wilt thou have me to do?" And such a spirit — the daily doing of God's will — will impart a serene loveliness to the character, and a simplicity of aim and purpose, that shall indeed make the heart at one with God and with Christ.

This will clothe us with righteousness and loveliness like a garment, and we shall be all unconscious save of our Master's presence, — too busy in finding out "how many simple ways there are to bless," to think anything about ourselves We shall love Christ more and more, and find our sympathies every day becoming more intense and unselfish.

> "To sojourn in the world, and yet apart;
> To dwell with God, and yet with man to feel,
> To bear about for ever in the heart
> The gladness that His spirit doth reveal"; —

here lies your true field of effort; here is a sphere to tax all your powers, to satisfy all your aspirations. "It is while we are walking in the way of duty that angel thoughts meet us." The kingdom of Heaven is within. Labor here earnestly and truly. Pray for the entire renewal, the sanctification, of your own heart; and hereafter you shall know that, through your life of faithful devotion to duty and of cheerful effort, through your confiding, humble faith and trust, through the pure and devout aspirations of your spirit, breathed indeed in secret, yet remembered on high, other souls have become sanctified through the truth.

Remember, too, the faithful words of a Christian poet: —

> "The trivial round, the common task,
> Will furnish all we ought to ask; —
> Room to deny ourselves; a road
> To bring us daily nearer God.

"Only, O Lord, in thy dear love
Fit us for perfect rest above;
And help us this, and every day,
To *live* more nearly as we pray."

LETTER X.

PRAYER.

I WISH, my dear friend, to bring distinctly and definitely before your mind at this time the subject of Prayer; for, if I am not mistaken, the "want of a steady and true progression in the Christian spirit and life," of which you complain, arises, in part at least, from erroneous views of the true nature and object of this important duty and privilege.

Apart from any other consideration, if you look merely at the teachings of Jesus on this subject, — from the commencement of his ministry, when crowds gathered around him and the poor and forsaken listened to his loving words of entreaty, when, with the chosen few, he withdrew to the calm stillness of Olivet, or uttered his teachings in that beloved home-circle which his presence has for ever sanctified to human thought, until in the shades and agony of Gethsemane, with the sorrows and sins of a world borne upon his heart, he turned yet again to the wearied and grief-stricken disciples, and in the solemn emphasis of that dark hour of woe, and as the last fervent utterance of earnest entreaty, bade them "watch and pray," — you cannot but feel that there is a solemnity and a reality connected with this duty, a power and a spiritual influence brought to bear upon the soul through the faithful use of this privilege, which you have hitherto regarded in too general and cursory a manner. It is true that you have formed the habit of daily prayer, and on no account would remit it, for there is a general, indistinct feeling in your soul that good in some way will result from it; but your thoughts, if definitely expressed, would sometimes utter themselves in this form: — "All events and purposes are clearly known to God; to him the future is present, no less than the past. He reads at a glance my whole inward being, my aims, desires, and intentions; he knows my secret sins and weaknesses, my strength of resistance and power of progress. As a God of love, of justice, and of power, he will impart to my soul all that it needs; he will give strength and grace, though I ask not for it; the circumstances of my outward life will of course be all ordered according to his infinite wisdom, and no thought or prayer of mine can change his fixed, unsearchable decrees. I will pray still, because somehow I feel as if neglecting a duty in omitting the stated exercises of devotion, and yet I really feel as if little positive good resulted from them.

"It is seldom that I feel that my prayers are directly answered, and when I read of, or meet with, those who seem to derive such actual comfort and hope from this spiritual communion with the unseen, there is a meaning in their words and expressions of trust which I have not yet fathomed. I acknowledge that there is an efficacy in lifting the soul to God, so far as it thus becomes more deeply impressed with a sense of its own sinfulness and dependence, and with God's perfect holiness and love, — so far as it learns more truly its own power of progress and advancement, and, through such self-excitation, is led to holier aims and desires; but more than this, I often cannot admit. It is true, that in seasons of sudden danger or deep anxiety I invoke the aid of God as by a natural impulse, and yet I know that my feeble prayers cannot change his fixed and general laws in the government of the world. There are moments, too, when my heart glows with love and holy gratitude to the great Giver of all good, and gladly do I utter my fervent thanksgiving and praise; but such an utterance can work no effect on the heart of the Infinite One. As a Christian duty, indeed, I still purpose and wish to continue the habit of prayer; but it is not a confiding, rejoicing act, or one from which I can trace any actual good results."

You may think, my friend, that I have overstated the case; but could you listen to the free utterances of some, calling themselves Christians, you would feel that even this is but a meagre outline of the actual condition of many hearts, of the want in many souls of any true, realizing faith in the efficacy of prayer.

These words may not all apply to your individual condition; but, if I am not mistaken, such feelings, only half acknowledged to yourself, and perhaps never actually expressed in words, have been the cause of many of your inward difficulties, have hindered your true progress, and kept you from those higher spiritual communings and enjoyments promised through Christ to every sincere seeker.

I would ask you, then, first of all, putting aside all mere philosophical speculations, and all endeavors to comprehend, with your limited and feeble capacities, the counsels of the Infinite God, to turn again to the simple teachings of Christ, to the words of him who came as the manifestation of the Father, and whose instructions you regard as of Divine authority. Reading such words, is there not some strange delusion in your mind, some perversion of feeling, that has led you to doubt and question the simple assurance of Christ? Have you not been led away by some fatal self-deception, debarring you from your true inheritance, and depriving you of your oft-desired peace and strength?

"If ye, being evil, know how to give good gifts unto your children, how much more shall your Heavenly Father give the holy spirit to them that *ask him!* Pray that ye enter not into temptation. Whatsoever ye shall ask in my name, that will I do. *Ask* and *receive*, that your joy may be full. Whatsoever ye shall ask in prayer, believing, ye *shall receive*." Can language be more emphatic than this? It is true there are two conditions annexed to this promised answer to prayer, but they are such as lie within the control of every sincere seeker, such as no true soul need fail of fulfilling.

As I have before said, God has not promised to give us the best gifts of his grace unless we *seek* and *ask* for them. It is not enough that we merely wish, or hope, or languidly desire them; but we must *ask*, — ask with earnestness, with sincerity, with a deep conviction of our need, with an intense longing to receive the petitions offered, — ask with the childlike earnestness that cannot be refused, unless the desired blessing be inconsistent with the soul's highest good. And we must ask, *believing* that we shall receive. There must be an entire faith and reliance on the simple promise of God, on his power, his willingness, his desire to grant to the soul all that it needs, all that a Father can bestow of love and blessing upon the heart of his child. When the disciples were astonished at the exhibition of the Divine power of Jesus, and he sought to impress their souls with the mighty influence of this inward principle of action, he did not directly answer the thoughts and questionings that must have arisen in their minds, but simply and emphatically said to them, "Have faith in God." And this same trust, belief, and unquestioning faith must we also possess, would we have poured into our souls those holy, divine influences, which, through Christ, are ever granted in answer to sincere prayer.

Cast away, then, your cold and specious reasonings, your sceptical doubts and unworthy questionings, and go to your Father with those earnest petitions and desires which can never fail of a true and full response. Cast away your sinful unbelief in the power of the Almighty to grant your requests, and believe that He who marshals all the mighty hosts of heaven, and calleth the stars by name, at whose fiat countless worlds and systems are brought into being, who looketh on the earth and it trembleth, and who holdeth the waters of the great deep as in the hollow of his hand, — believe that He, who knoweth the end from the beginning, can so adapt the secret workings of his providence, and the holy influences of his spirit, as to answer the prayers of the humblest of his children, and to meet the faintest heavenward desires and longings of the youngest heart.

It is true that God knows that you have need of these blessings, and that he bestows upon you countless favors without your asking; yet he has seen fit to grant these special influences, and this inward strength and help, only where the soul so longs and desires for them as to *ask* for them. And is not such a condition reasonable and just? Is it not in accordance with our whole earthly experience? Is there aught unreasonable or strange in such a simple command, — "*Ask*, that ye may receive"?

But you say, "God is immutable, and no word or prayer of mine can change his unalterable decrees." True, with him is no variableness, neither shadow of turning; but has not your view of the Divine nature, exalted as you think it to be, limited him in his power of will and of action? Taking your stand upon the highest plane of spiritual truth, as you imagine, and embracing the whole creation and government of the universe under the "general laws" of nature, as you term them, have you not in reality circumscribed and limited that Infinite, Eternal Power? Have you not vainly set bounds to his Almightiness? Have you not in reality made your own feebleness the measure of his Omnipotence? If, as we believe, his laws and purposes are eternal, are they not so vast, so comprehensive, as to *include* the care of the least of his creatures, the answer to every secret aspiration, every sigh of penitence, every sincere and earnest prayer? You imagine, perhaps, that in your view alone the Divine nature is truly exalted and honored, forgetting that with him there is "no high, no low, no great, no small," and that there can be nothing more derogatory than to limit his modes of action to our finite thought and comprehension. Taking the simple declaration of Jesus, as he pointed to the lilies of the field and the fowls of the air, and taught the love and constant care of God over the least of his outward works, shall we sinfully doubt that he has so organized the great structure of the moral universe as to be able to adapt his peculiar blessings to every changing want of the immortal soul, — that conscious spirit through which alone we hold communion with Him?

Do not all the teachings of Christ assure us that he comes to every penitent, waiting soul with the *peculiar* ministries of his grace, granting his favors, his special gifts, even as the heart turns to him and confides in his promises of forgiving love? "Whatsoever ye shall ask in my name, that *will I do*, that the Father may be glorified in the Son."

But you say: "I have surely no reason to ask for any merely temporal, outward blessings; the circumstances of my life are all ordered by the Divine will, and these can form no part of real prayer."

Yet have not these very circumstances a constant reflex influence over your inward being; and can they then be, however humble, a matter of indifference, to be excluded from the thoughts in the hour of secret devotion? Christ himself has taught us to pray for our daily bread; and while we ask most earnestly for that living Bread of which he who eateth shall never hunger, surely we may also pray for that necessary nourishment of the bodily life, which ever cometh from Him who feeds the fowls of the air, and hears the young ravens when they cry.

How far and to what degree the discipline of the outward life, health and sickness, joy and sorrow, prosperity and adversity, may be arranged or modified, if I may so speak, in answer to the prayer of faith, we know not. Yet if such prayers are offered in sincerity and trust, with an implicit reliance on the goodness and providence of God, with faith that, whatever may be the result, it will surely be for the soul's best and eternal good, then they are not in vain. They bring the soul into a truer harmony with the Divine will, taking away all restless impatience, and leading it to feel, that, through these outward surroundings, trials, and obstacles, it is to be led through the mere vestibule into the holy inward sanctuary of the temple of the Most High.

They lead us, also, to see the hand of Providence in all the circumstances of our daily life; thus blending the thought of God with the most common scenes, and hallowing the daily routine of duty by His ever-watchful presence. And who knows how often danger may be averted, and blessings bestowed, in *direct* answer to the prayer of the believing soul?

However dim our faith, however distrustful our cold and unbelieving hearts, let us not limit the power of the Almighty, nor set bounds to His ways among the children of men! Let us not vainly imagine that the deepest philosophy can fathom the wonderful mysteries of the spirit-world, or comprehend its vast and beneficent laws of cause and effect, and spiritual influence; but, accepting the simple words of the Redeemer, "Ask, and ye shall receive," let us bow in conscious humility, and, opening our souls to the influences of the Spirit, ask in faith, that we may receive the promised blessing.

But you say again, "Often I derive little real help or comfort from my prayers. I offer them from a sense of duty; but I find no special help resulting from them, and in consequence there is little joy or peace in the exercise."

Now, the answer to prayer may be regarded both as special and general. We may be able to trace its immediate results, and may feel and know that our petitions are answered, either from the inward testimony of the spirit, the conscious help and strength imparted in the hour of temptation and in the performance of duty, and the peace which passeth understanding that fills the soul when the whole inward being is in harmony with the Divine will; or from those open, direct, unmistakable answers to fervent prayer, which cannot but arrest the attention even of the thoughtless and indifferent. And, on the other hand, there may be no immediate sense of the promised response, and yet deep in the soul, perhaps even below the region of distinct consciousness, the secret influences of the Divine spirit will so act upon the whole being as to change, regenerate, and sanctify it, and thus more than answer its most earnest petitions, though the individual may often be unable to trace the distinct process by which such renewal is effected.

Again, do we pray for some peculiar blessing, and at the same time ask for a deeper and holier faith in God and Christ? May not the better gift be granted only through the denial of the lesser good? May not the outward blessing which we crave be often withheld even from sincere prayer, that the spirit of an unfaltering faith and an unwavering trust may be implanted in the most secret recesses of the soul?

But you say that your prayers do not bring to your soul the light and satisfaction you desire. How, then, do you offer them? What is their spirit, and what your true purpose in praying?

Is there a real earnestness on your part, a deep sincerity, a heart-felt desire to receive the blessings asked? When you pray to be made more humble, to have all self-confidence taken from you, to be strong only through the help that Christ imparts, do you *really*, in your inmost soul, desire that such should be your profound experience? or are you still cherishing some secret pride, some vain self-reliance, some desire to uphold your rights, and your pride or honor in the eyes of the world, however this may conflict with the known law of Christ? Do you pray for a more gentle, forgiving, forbearing temper, and yet at the first provocation harbor unkind thoughts and resentful feelings, and excuse your ready yielding to temptation by saying that the occasion justifies such righteous indignation? Do you ask in the morning to be filled with the Divine spirit and guided by the Divine will, and yet throughout the day seek only your own pleasures, and give all your thoughts to mere business, dress, or fashion? Do you pray that God and Christ may abide with you, and yet close those secret avenues to your soul through which alone the holy spirit may enter, by an undue absorption in the transient, passing things of earth and of time? Test the true spirit of your prayers; try your life by them. Know whether they are really sincere; and if you find that you have indeed been faithless on your part, then question not vainly the Divine omnipotence and love, but, with a child's confession and trust, go to your Father, and renewedly seek, in humble and sincere penitence, the desired help and strength.

Then, too, let me counsel you to be faithful to those means which are always a help to true prayer; for this act is at once the loftiest and highest, and yet the most simple, that can ever engage the human soul,—demanding thought, energy, faith, and earnestness. It is the human holding converse with the Divine, the finite with the Infinite and Eternal. Let the season of prayer be preceded by thought and devout contemplation, by communion with your own soul, and a renewed recognition of your entire dependence upon the Author and Upholder of your being. Feel the sacredness of that Divine presence before which you bow; let no vague, unmeaning phrases pass your lips; but in lowly self-abasement and in simple faith offer your petitions, not in any set form of words, but in the sincere outpouring of your most secret desires and wants. Think not that any occurrences of the passing day, any duties however lowly, any temptations however slight, any joys or griefs however seemingly trivial, are too minute or too humble to bring before your Father and your Saviour. Our prayers are sometimes unmeaning, because we deal so much in generalities. We offer petitions for the world at large, that sin may be put away and the kingdom of righteousness established; we pray that God's will may be done throughout the whole earth; and at the same time our own hearts are in a state of aught but submission under some trifling inconvenience or personal suffering, or our minds are filled with some petty vexation that has ruffled our tempers or tried our patience; and these so-called trifles we vainly seek to hide from the eye of the All-searching One, asking for blessings in general, and not for what we *really* want at the moment. "But were God in Christ known and regarded as the soul's familiar friend; were every trouble of the heart, as it rises, breathed into his bosom; were it felt that there is not one of the smallest of life's trifles that has not been permitted by Him, and permitted for some specific good purpose to the soul, how much more heart-work would there be in prayer! How daily, how constant, might it become!"

Accustom yourself, also, to inward ejaculatory prayer. When your hands are busy, or when enjoying the wonderful beauties of the outward world, or exercising your physical powers, or even when the mind is engaged in business or intellectual pursuits, let there be the frequent turning of the soul to God, the secret prayer for strength and guidance, breathed in the sacred language of Scripture, or the devout utterance of some familiar hymn; and so let every occupation, every duty and pleasure, lead you nearer and yet nearer to the Source of truth and life. Thus alone will you learn to feel as a blessed reality the Father's love, presence, and sustaining help; thus alone will you enter into that holy and ceaseless communing with the Divine Spirit which is the only true life of the soul.

"Come, in thy pleading spirit, down
To us, who for thy coming stay;
Of all thy gifts we ask but one,
We ask the constant power to pray.
O, grant us, Lord, this great request;
Thou canst not then deny the rest."

While you thus seek to "pray without ceasing," and offer in faith earnest petitions for your own spiritual life and guidance, let me ask whether your prayers are sufficiently those of intercession, or whether there is not a covert, baneful spirit of selfishness at times inwoven even with your most devotional moods and highest desires? Have you habitually remembered your duty and your privilege, while seeking spiritual favors for yourself, to bear others on your heart to the throne of grace? You may possess but the one talent, so far as your direct influence over others is concerned; your sphere of duty may be limited and confined; sickness may cripple your active powers, or circumstances compel you to expend all your time and efforts in providing for the bare necessities of life; but, thank God, none of these things can bind the soul, or repress its immortal aspirations, or close the avenues of secret prayer. Christ ever abides with you, heaven opens before you, immortality unfolds its visions of glory, joy, and ceaseless progress; and whose but the All-seeing Eye can trace these secret spiritual ministries, those purer aims, holier desires, and more devout purposes, awakened in other souls through the all-prevailing power of fervent intercession?

A faithful and devoted missionary, in a distant and foreign land, thus wrote to a Christian friend, from his arduous field of labor: "Perhaps you cannot do more for the cause of Christ than to set apart stated and frequent seasons for *special* supplication in our behalf. It is not by the number and strength of missionaries that the great work is to be accomplished; but through the intercession of the children of God, the holy spirit will be given. This is a part of your appropriate work, — allow me to say, a *great part*, — a talent put into your hands for which you must render an account."

Our prayers deepen in intensity and fervor in proportion to their individuality; and if we feel that true interest in the spiritual welfare of others that leads us to desire, above all things else, their redemption from sin, and their personal consecration to the Master's service, will not our petitions be freighted with new ardor and earnestness, — will not the secret hour of devotion be often prolonged as we remember the promise of the Eternal through his Son, "Ask, and ye shall receive"? Are there not friends and kindred, the young, the tempted, the suffering, the sinning, all around us, who thus need our prayers for help, and strength, and spiritual life? Does not the cause of Christ languish in many of our churches, and religious faith grow dim, and earnestness die away, because the prayers of Christians are so faint and few that his "kingdom may come"? So far as you are able to unite at stated times with others, whether in public or private, in these petitions for mutual help and spiritual strength, deem it ever your privilege so to do, thus weaving closer the bonds of a spiritual interest and sympathy with the sincere followers of Christ; but if debarred from such communion, neglect not your own personal duty and privilege, in offering those secret prayers of intercession, breathed only for the ear of Him who ever hears the faintest whisper of the true and earnest heart.

Finally, you have constant and imperative need of this vital spirit of prayer to sustain your own soul in the daily, hourly conflict with temptation and sin, and to cherish a living spirit of gratitude and trust.

"Rugged and thorny is the path
  Marked for the Christian's race,
And thou wilt deviate and fall
  Without God's strengthening grace.
Then, while He fills the mercy-seat,
  Be thou no stranger there:
The heavenly manna must be sought
  Daily, through fervent prayer."

Seek, then, faithfully the sure and sustaining influences of the spirit, promised and pledged to the soul through the Redeèmer. Receive each spiritual help and blessing through him as the one Mediator. Look to him as the faithful Intercessor, and remember his parting words of peace, strength, and promise, rolling back from the soul the clouds of doubt, fear, and uncertainty, and shedding over it the calm radiance of celestial peace: — "Hitherto ye have asked nothing in my name. *Ask, and ye shall receive*, that your joy may be full."

LETTER XI.

SPIRITUAL TRIALS.

Your last letter, my dear friend, assures me that you are truly seeking to lead the life of the Christian, and are earnestly striving for a deeper and purer faith; yet there are doubts and difficulties in your mind which you hardly know how to interpret or meet, — a darkness which often hides from you the Father's reconciled countenance, and robs you of all true peace.

To point out to you the meaning of these difficulties, and to show you how even such trials may be made conducive to your highest spiritual good, will be now my aim. The subjects upon which I shall touch are such as peculiarly require inward scrutiny and the concentrated attention of the spiritual powers; for the faith which you need and desire is, from its very nature, wholly spiritual, and can never be attained by any outward process, or by any effort of the intellectual powers alone.

We live too much in externals, and are too readily satisfied when the daily routine of life is, on the whole, comfortable and satisfying, forgetting the unfathomed depths of being, the mysteries of the world within, which occasionally startle us from our slumber of indifference and heartless peace, as some strange, unforeseen event, some wonderful, providential dealing, some sudden light from the Divine word or the ever-present spirit, pierces the most secret recesses of the soul, revealing its intricate windings, its want and destitution, its weakness and its strength, its helplessness in self-confidence, and its power in an entire self-renunciation.

Well has it been said: "In man's deepest consciousness, read sometimes clearly and sometimes dimly, is the subject-matter of a Paradise Lost and a Paradise Regained, which the seers and bards of humanity have struggled to articulate distinctly in prophecy and song. Only when the things of immortality become mere matters of tradition, and not subjective realities, man conceives this drama as enacted in some far-off and imaginary heavens, and not where alone it can be found, — in himself."

Something of these inward trials, something of these struggles, amounting at times even to anguish of soul, you have felt, and the conflict has been the harder because you have had few or none to understand and to sympathize with your deepest wants.

Many there are who virtually regard the external circumstances of life — sickness, poverty, uncongenial pursuits and labors, loss of property, bereavements — as the only trials of life, and would hardly comprehend the language of one who speaks of such as are wholly inward and spiritual. " For the natural man receiveth not the things of the spirit of God; neither can he know them, because they are spiritually discerned."

Not that I would overlook, or regard as of little account, what is usually termed the outward discipline of life, requiring as it does the truest Christian faith to meet it with a cheerful trust and a holy submission. But appealing now to your own consciousness, I would ask, Is this all? When life has seemed the most joyous, and external circumstances the most propitious, has there not often been the deepest trial and the most intense struggle in the inward spirit?

Judging from your last letter and my knowledge of your past spiritual experience, your state of mind might be expressed in a confession like this: " I am conscious of having made the distinct choice of the religious life, of having sought to follow Jesus as my only guide and to know him as my Saviour. I have striven to feel my personal relations to him, to be faithful in prayer and the study of the Scriptures, and diligent in duty. But again and again does the solemn question recur, Am I born again? Ought I to regard myself as entitled to those promises made to the children of God? Failing so often in duty, do I truly belong to Christ and share in his covenant of love? I have not that realizing faith in God and in Christ which, in my better moments, I desire. At times, there even seems no reality in their being, — heaven appears afar off and immortality a dream. I pray, but cannot feel the Father's loving presence. I long to hear the still, small voice, but there is only silence. I meditate, but doubts arise as to the reality of the themes of revelation. I ponder the life of the divine Redeemer, but no glow of warm emotion suffuses my soul, and I cannot feel the love and devotion I desire. I seek to cherish a deeper faith, but often the words of revelation seem to have no personal application; and when I am alone, in the hour of retirement and prayer, often all appears to my spirit blank, vague, and unmeaning. There are times, indeed, when faith grows clear and bright, and, with renewed courage and hope, I can press on in the conflict; but again and again do these darker seasons recur, and, weary and disheartened, I am tempted to yield to self-indulgence and to give up all effort. How, then, am I to meet these struggles, these trials of religious confidence? How satisfy this restless yearning for a more abiding and conscious reconciliation, and a truer fellowship with Christ?"

I reply: If you are indeed conscious of a true consecration of yourself to God through Christ, and of looking to his spirit for guidance and help, if you are faithful in prayer, then understand that these darker hours, these seasons of coldness and doubt and inward restlessness, are the *trying of your faith*, the test of your sincerity, the divinely appointed means of your growth in the spiritual life.

Some there are who need chiefly the varied and changing discipline of the outward life to render them fit for the kingdom of Heaven; but others are to be purified through inward trial, through secret and severe struggles unknown save to the eye of the All-seeing, and are thus alone prepared to receive the crown of life which the Master has promised to those who abide faithful even amid the darkness, and who are called upon cheerfully to bear his cross, knowing that it will soon bear them beyond the scenes of trial, conflict, and doubt, to the unveiled presence of the Father and the Saviour.

In such inward struggles, the first essential condition of our attaining to any true peace and faith of the soul is, that we become thoroughly conscious of our weakness and our needs; that we feel the absolute necessity of giving up all self-confidence, and relying solely on the Father's help and mercy as manifested in Christ. Now, in these trials of religious confidence, there is doubtless some need within your soul, some unhealthy tendency, some secret destitution, that can be remedied only through a purely spiritual discipline; and it is wonderful to observe how many different and peculiar ways the Father has of leading us to himself. Now he aids us by imparting the clear, full light of his countenance, and again, in equal love, by withholding the conscious sense of his presence and favor; now, by suffusing the soul with gladness, joy, and peace, and then by permitting doubt, sorrow, and uneasiness; now, by crowning the life with success and prosperity, and again, in like mercy, darkening every earthly prospect by disappointment, suffering, and sorrow; now, by giving the full assurance of his forgiveness and reconciling mercy in Christ, and then, in equal love, clouding the spiritual vision, and hiding the full rays of his countenance; now, by laying on us the cross, and then by holding forth the crown; yet always with the same Divine wisdom, always with the same great purpose of infinite love, — to lead the soul to an unwavering trust, a childlike confidence, a perfect faith.

In the words of another: "You have been years wandering, unfitting yourself for spiritual peace, because out of harmony with God, who demands the supreme devotion of your soul. What right have you to expect to spring, at one bound, into the complete restoration of every disordered faculty? It ought to be enough, if, your face being firmly turned towards your Father in Heaven, he lifts, little by little, the veil that hides the full splendor of his presence. What you are to learn by your present discontent is, that you are not sufficient to yourself, but must look above yourself; that you cannot guide yourself, but must beseech the Spirit to guide you; that you, being finite, cannot grasp infinite things, but must let the Saviour reach up for you, show you where your uncertain hand shall lay hold on the rod and staff, and make you one with him. But what wonder, if, before the Father introduces you into the full joy of believing, or the rewards of obedience, he first tries your faith? Be sure, that no otherwise can you have that *faithful spirit* of which Christian disciples are made."

But you ask, Why is this discipline my peculiar appointment? Why is not a hopeful trust and assurance granted to me, even as to others? Why these secret struggles, to be met only in silence? Why this darkness of spirit, often clouding every joyous scene, and dimming every future hope? Ah! question not vainly the appointed discipline of the All-wise and All-merciful! Rather let the words of the Redeemer be an all-sufficient response: "What I do thou knowest not now, but thou shalt know hereafter."

Could we see the end from the beginning,— were the results of our probation all clearly mirrored before us,— what room would there be for the exercise of faith? But in these inward struggles, no less than in the outward discipline of life, we must still seek the Saviour's spirit, and breathe his prayer of submission, "Father, thy will be done."

And does not the whole revelation of God through Christ assure us that the great end of life, and the true meaning of all its varied discipline, is to produce, and test, and purify our faith, until it becomes an unchanging, unwavering, all-conquering Trust?

You long for a deeper assurance, for a more conscious personal relationship to your Saviour, for a more realizing sense of things unseen; but with your longings and desires, has there not sometimes been mingled a secret restlessness and impatience? Have you not forgotten those words of the Psalmist, far more enduring and significant than all his regal glory and authority, and pregnant with an immortal life and power: "Rest in the Lord, and *wait patiently* for him." Abiding *in* him, have you been willing to *wait* his own time for a fuller revelation, for more quickening influences from his spirit, no less than to strive and to pray for them?

"The crown of patience cannot be received where there has been no suffering. If thou refuse to suffer, thou refusest to be crowned; but if thou wish to be crowned, thou must fight manfully and suffer patiently."

Longing to feel more truly the Saviour's presence and love, hear as if from his own lips the words of assurance: "Let not thy heart be troubled, neither let it be afraid. Believe in me, whose redeeming power has overcome the world, and place all thy confidence in my mercy. I am often nearest thee when thou thinkest me at the greatest distance; and when thou hast given up all as lost in darkness, the light of peace is ready to break upon thee."

Knowing your own insufficiency, and having the Divine promise that, in God's own time and way, the holy spirit *will* be given to every heart that truly seeks it, why will you not quietly rely on this assurance with an undoubting faith, and willingly bear the cross, which can alone lead to the ascension mount of a clearer faith and vision?

"O Way for all that live! heal us by pain and loss;
Fill all our years with toil, and bless us with thy rod:
Thy bonds bring wider freedom; climbing by the cross
Wins that bright height where looms the city of our God."

There is also another subtle tendency in your soul, indistinctly recognized by yourself, and unknown to some, but which has doubtless marred your progress and often clouded your spiritual vision; namely, "The temptation of longing more earnestly for rest than for faithful submission. You have heard that there is joy in believing, and so you undertake to believe for the sake of the joy. You desire a comfortable and quiet mind; and this, though it is a far nobler thirst than that of the senses, is still, if it is too strong, tainted with selfishness, and wanting in faith. As there is a spiritual pride, so there is a spiritual luxury, and the appetite that lusts after it is one of the subtle enemies that beset those who have passed out of the lowest stage of conscience into the second. There is an ambition to do something as out of your own self, for the delight of approving yourself, which is nothing else than self-righteousness. The mercenary tendency to offer God your good works as a price for purchasing an allowance of self-complacency, is one that needs to be watched by sincere seekers after the liberty and nobleness of true devotion. It defeats its own end. Peace never comes in that way; nothing does but discontent and confusion. Peace comes swiftest when you seek it as an end least. Seek purity, seek renewal of heart and life, seek harmony with God, seek the society of Christ as a Saviour and Intercessor for you, and Peace, in God's good time, will come of itself."

Do you reply, "I acknowledge all of this to be true in my better moments, yet in the hours of clouded faith I am impatient, and long to comprehend at once the reality of things unseen?"

Remember, then, now and ever, the one great end of all this spiritual discipline. Remember that often we must be buffeted in our highest desires before we become thoroughly humble and altogether Christ's.

Remember, too, that though peace and joy in believing are spoken of as the ultimate fruits of the Spirit, they are not necessarily to be regarded as the direct and *immediate* results.

A full assurance of faith blesses the seeking, waiting soul, as indeed the gift of God, — but as a gift, withheld in a measure from some, only that a greater and more enduring good may be granted. From you it may be withheld, in God's inscrutable wisdom; but will it not be enough, if, when this earthly scene is passed, and this earthly veil withdrawn, you come forth from the furnace seven times purified, a vessel meet for the Master's use?

The very longing and desire you have for a deeper and more realizing faith, show that you are not wholly destitute of its power.

> "He that wants faith, and apprehends a grief
> *Because* he wants it, has a true belief;
> And he who grieves because his grief's so small
> Has a true grief, and the best faith of all."

In the words of Thomas à Kempis, that wonderful master of the heart's deep secrets, "Think not thyself abandoned when I permit tribulation to come upon thee for a season, or suspend the consolations thou art always fondly desiring; for this is the narrow way to the kingdom of Heaven; and it is more expedient for my servants to be exercised with many sufferings, than to enjoy that perpetual rest and peace which they would choose for themselves. I, who know the hidden thoughts of thy heart, and the depth of the evil that is in it, know that thy salvation depends upon being sometimes left in the full perception of thy own sins and weakness; lest, in the undisturbed prosperity of the spiritual life, thou shouldest exalt thyself for what is not thy own, and take complacence in vain conceit of perfection, to which man of himself cannot attain. . . . . The advancement of spiritual life depends, not upon the enjoyment of consolation, but upon bearing the want of it with resignation, humility, and patience, so as not to relinquish prayer, or remit any of thy accustomed holy exercises."

But you say again, "I would willingly bear this want of assurance and this trial of faith, could I only feel that I indeed belong to Christ; but when I seek within, for the marks of the regenerate spirit, I find myself so far from the true Christian standard, that, at times, I dare not believe that I am 'born again.'"

In reply, let me again ask if you are not looking too much to the efficacy of your own works and your own attainments, and too little to the cross of Christ. Have you not still some latent thought of meriting the Divine approval, instead of relying solely on the free mercy of God, pledged to the soul in the suffering and risen Saviour?

Do you not still cherish a lingering doubt of the words of promise, instead of joyfully and thankfully receiving them into the soul, as the very help and strength you need, so freely and fully vouchsafed to you? "He that cometh to me I will in no wise cast out. Come unto me, all ye who are weary and heavy-laden, and I will give you rest. Herein is love, not that we loved God, but that he loved us, and sent his Son to be the propitiation for our sins." Look not within with such anxious self-questioning, but turn to the cross and seek there a more confiding and cheerful trust, and, relying on God's love and goodness, let it be your daily prayer, that whether by suffering or comfort, by grief or peace, through darkness or light, you may be so chastened and renewed as to be wholly His; that you may be able to say and to feel in all things, "Thy will be done."

"In meek obedience to the heavenly Teacher,
Thy weary soul can find its only peace;
Seeking no aid from any human creature,
Looking to God alone for its release.

"And He *will* come in his own time and power,
To set his earnest-hearted children free;
Watch only through this dark and painful hour,
And the bright morning yet will dawn for thee."

"Know then," in the emphatic words of another, — "know that the two powers that this slow trying of your faith and religious constancy are meant to develop in your soul, are *humbler prayers*, and a more patient *feeling after and following after Christ.* These together are faith; and their certain end, in God's own time, will be peace and assurance."

Know too that you are not alone in these secret conflicts. The spiritual experience of the pure and the faithful in all ages and climes assures us that through much tribulation must we enter into the kingdom of Heaven. From the rapt musings and utterances of inspired prophets; from the lowly self-abasement and humiliation of the Hebrew bard, as he swept the strings of his harp in mournful unison with his own self-accusing and penitent spirit; from the self-upbraiding of the faithless disciple, and the deep and mighty spiritual struggles of the greatest of the Apostles; from faithful witnesses to the truth in those earlier times; from the confessions of Augustine, and the pleading eloquence of Chrysostom; from the retirement of Jerome and the convent of Theresa, and from that deep voice of inward conflict and agony resounding over the wastes of the desert, and echoing from mountain caves and solitary groves and the deepest recesses of the wilderness; from all the faithful and true in the midst of sorrow and doubt and temptation; from Luther's cell, the scene of his mightiest struggle and victory; from Loyola's couch of suffering, and from Chalmers's chamber of illness; from Bunyan's prison of conflict, from Brainerd's wilderness abode, and from Edwards's midnight study; from Fenelon's meditations on the deep things of the inward life, and from many a redeemed and purified spirit in quiet home-circles of love and peace, — comes one united voice of faith and of hope, bidding us doubt not, and despond not, but strive as they have striven, and trust as they have trusted; assuring us, that for us too, in God's own time, the clouds of earth may all be rolled away, and, in the fulness of His conscious presence, we may receive for ever "the open vision for the written word."

I have spoken of trials of religious confidence. There are yet many others which you have already experienced to some extent, or which, if life be spared, must soon be yours: trials of sickness, of bereavement, of parting with friends, of sudden changes and unexpected reverses, of anxious days and weary nights and lonely hours, — trials that will test to the utmost the reality of your faith, the sincerity of your obedience, and the depth of your submission. As in the more secret struggles of the soul, so in these you must go forth alone to the conflict, and, like the prophet of old, must tread the wine-press alone; for no human friend, however near and dear, can fully comprehend your soul, or understand the peculiar sorrows and trials that at times bow your spirit in grief and in agony. And yet you are not alone, if the Father is with you; not alone, if beneath you are the Everlasting arms; not alone, if the Saviour's voice whispers amid the darkness, "It is I, be not afraid," and to the surging waves of grief says, "Peace, be still"; not alone, if the Redeemer's hand is laid upon your brow in blessing, and the pulses of your throbbing heart are stilled by his holy benediction, "Peace I leave with you; my peace I give unto you; not as the world giveth, give I unto you: let not your heart be troubled, neither let it be afraid."

From the night-watches on Olivet, from the garden of Gethsemane, and the cross on Calvary, have come the Christian's hope and trust; and in the light of the Saviour's countenance suffering is for evermore transfigured, and trial and grief made radiant with a heavenly brightness and joy.

God grant that you may so meet the varied discipline of life, and so seek its one great end, that through every new trial of your faith you may be brought to a more trusting confidence in your Father, and to a more assured repose on your Saviour's love ; receiving, at length, the end of your faith, even the salvation of your soul.

LETTER XII.

THE DAILY LIFE.

Having spoken to you of the great spiritual meaning of life, and of its varied spiritual discipline and experience, and believing that you are sincerely striving to walk in that narrow path of Christian obedience which the Master has marked before you, it might seem unnecessary for me to refer to any of the details of daily conduct, which I might leave to the cognizance of your own inward convictions of duty, and the judgment of your own conscience.

Yet when I remember how many who enter upon the Christian course fail in the race, and grow weary and disheartened, through the routine of daily toil and care, and the constant friction of little troubles and vexations, or rest midway in the course, making no definite progress, neglecting the cultivation of their powers, and falling into habits of self-indulgence, selfishness, and worldliness, I feel that the young pilgrim needs every help and defence which Christian counsel, sympathy, and love can place around him, to aid and sustain him in the narrow path of life. Let me then speak to you freely and simply, trusting that my words will be received with kindness, though they may contain no new or exciting truths.

If I am not mistaken, your true aim and sincere desire in every better moment is to be in heart and life a follower of Christ, a true and faithful disciple of your divine Master ; and such an aim and desire includes at once the entire consecration of all your powers to his service, — your powers of heart and mind, your opportunities of doing good and exerting a Christian influence, the employment of your time, the use of your means, the improvement of every opportunity of self-culture, the doing of God's will and not your own, in things little no less than great. You have given yourself to your Master's service, and simple, child-like obedience to his commands is his one requirement. You are no longer to consult your own ease and pleasure and self-indulgence, but to merge each selfish, lower thought in the desire to conform the spirit wholly to the Divine will.

You have chosen Christ as your only true guide, and are therefore never to compare your life and character with the imperfect attainments or the low standard of those around you, but to look only to the spirit and life of Him who alone has given the perfect example which you are to follow. "Be ye perfect, even as your Father in heaven is perfect." "Be ye holy, for I am holy."

I do not ask whether such a spirit and such a life is an easy attainment, but I do ask whether there is not, at times, a secret and baneful tendency in your soul to rest satisfied with a low standard of obedience, with a half-way compliance with many of the Divine laws, with a readiness to exclude some of the pursuits and business of the daily life from comparison with the strict requirements of your only perfect standard and guide?

As to the regulation of your whole inward being, the control of your thoughts, wishes, and desires, do you habitually and daily bring these under the cognizance of the great laws of accountability, or do you often remain content if in outward act the life has been in any good measure conformed to the dictates of truth and of duty? Have you remembered that thoughts are truly the deeds of the soul, and, when your hands have been busily occupied, have you watched their swiftly changing current, seeking to keep it pure and clear, — a transparent stream of holy desires, and pure affections, and noble deeds, in which the Divine image may be truly mirrored? Have you endeavored at such times so to regulate and control them as to turn them to useful subjects of contemplation, reviewing the books you have read, the sermons and lectures you have heard, strengthening your judgment, attention, and reasoning powers by seeking abstract themes of thought and inquiry, tracing the guiding care and love of God in all the varied circumstances of your own life, his providential dealings with your soul, his greatness, power, and wisdom, as displayed in the works of creation, his holiness and love as manifested in Christ the Saviour? In whatever manual labor, or routine of toil, you have been engaged, if your thoughts have been left free to range at will, has the day been truly improved so long as no conscious effort has been made thus to deepen, enlarge, and purify the fountains of your inward being, — so long as God has not thus been in all your thoughts?

Your affections, too, are to be fixed supremely upon what is unseen and heavenly; and if your love to God and to Christ be sincere and heartfelt, love to your fellow-men of every age and condition will daily grow deeper and stronger within your soul. The first commandment cannot be truly fulfilled without a faithful obedience to the second; and these pure and holy affections, this tender regard for others' welfare, this desire to live for their good, and not for mere selfish aims and purposes, this divine charity that thinketh no evil, and would transform the intended injury into a heavenly blessing, this tender, gentle love, stronger than death, and shedding its halo of celestial radiance over every darker scene of earthly care, trial, and sorrow, — this can bless the soul and transform it into the Divine image, only through the daily exercise of loving thoughts and deeds, through gentle words, and the cultivation of each holy affection. Your sympathies, too, if your spirit truly be conformed to your Master's, will be in harmony with all that is pure, true, and heavenly, and will readily flow forth at every call of benevolence and charity, not wasting themselves in mere vague wishes or expressions of pity that require no self-sacrifice, but manifesting their truth and their reality by the tender regard, the ready deed, the open hand, and the gentle word of kindness. Many there are who will mourn over fictitious tales of sorrow and of suffering, and even pride themselves upon their tenderness of feeling, whose presence never cheers the chamber of sickness, or lights the dark abode of grief, or gladdens the home of suffering and poverty; who never seek to bear another's burden of care or anxiety, to comfort the lonely heart, or impart peace to the mourning spirit. And yet such would fain call themselves Christian disciples.

But while you seek to follow your Saviour in the earnest cultivation of every pure and holy emotion, in the quickening of every feeling of kindly sympathy, let me guard you against any undue longing for receiving this in return. There is in many souls a subtile craving, a morbid yearning to receive full and entire sympathy from those with whom they are daily associated; and where this is united with a shrinking, sensitive temperament, it often engenders a sickly selfishness, and a spirit of exaction that is seldom satisfied with the simple courtesies and kindnesses of the daily life, but is ever demanding a larger share of love and of sympathy. It places self first, and requires love in order to bestow it, instead of letting the affections flow forth in genial kindness toward all of God's children, and loving them in and through Christ.

Yet it needs not wide experience, nor the discipline of many years to assure us, that there are seasons in the lives of all, when, so far as regards human aid and sympathy, we must breast the conflict alone; that there are secret desires and heavenly aspirations, earnest longings and grave doubts, heavy anxieties and restless yearnings for a truer peace and hope, which must be combated only in the secret solitude of the soul, and which the nearest and dearest can never fully comprehend.

But why should we shrink even from this discipline, — to some, the sternest in life? Why refuse to drink even of this cup? Why not, rather, make it the blessed means of leading us to a more entire trust in the Father, and a more implicit reliance on the Saviour's constant love, tenderness, and sympathy? Why not let it teach us to live out of ourselves, by living wholly to God and to Christ? Why not so purify this craving for human sympathy, and so discipline this painful sensitiveness of the inward nature, that every pure and loving affection shall twine only the more certainly around the tree of life, — that every sensitive fibre of the soul's secret being shall have its firm and enduring root in the Rock of Ages?

The busy world moves on; day follows day, and the restless tide of human life sweeps by us, little heeding whether we are borne along by the current, or whether we silently disappear beneath its surging waves. Yet not unnoticed do we move on; one Eye there is, which marks the sparrow's fall, and no thought of the child's spirit escapes that searching glance. And shall it not be enough to the heart longing for sympathy to know that it may be enfolded for ever in the arms of everlasting love, to believe that the Infinite One has manifested himself in the Saviour, to pledge to the soul that love, and to draw it nearer to himself? With this conscious sympathy, yield up, then, all disquiet. Repose on the bosom of eternal love, and the spirit of trust shall fill your soul with a gentle, self-sacrificing love, that shall find it ever far more blessed to give than to receive.

Rest in the Saviour's tender sympathy, and though, in the secret recesses of the soul, deep calleth unto deep, and no human voice responds to the earnest cry of longing desire, he who fathomed every depth of earthly trial and sorrow will be with you, and in his presence and his love shall you find peace.

> "O holy trust! O endless sense of rest!
> Like the beloved John
> To lay the head upon the Saviour's breast,
> And thus to journey on!"

Your time is also to be regarded as a sacred and holy trust, for which you are to render a strict account. However pressing may be the routine of daily business, care, or toil, some portion of each day should be sacredly set apart for spiritual thought, meditation, and prayer. He who thinks the use of all such seasons superseded by obeying the Apostle's command to "pray without ceasing," will doubtless end in not praying at all, and sinking into carelessness, worldliness, and indifference. The spirit no less than the body needs its regular seasons of refreshment and strengthening; and while so much care, time, and thought are given to the supply of the bodily wants, is there not some inward disorder, some spiritual sickness, if you grudge the hour set apart for the special nourishment of your immortal nature, — if you derive little enjoyment or help from your regular seasons of devotion? If your interest in spiritual themes, your hours of religious meditation, your seasons of prayer, lose their attraction for you, then pause, and faithfully examine the true state of your soul, and turn again ere it be too late; retrace the forsaken path, and in lowly confession again implore the help of the Spirit to break the bonds of indifference and worldliness.

However occupied the day may be, let a certain portion of it be also sacredly set apart for the cultivation of your intellectual powers. Many make it an excuse, that they have no time for mere mental pursuits, and therefore make no effort to add to their knowledge, or to strengthen and develop their powers of memory, reason, and judgment. Yet even fifteen minutes a day, faithfully and systematically used, would give one in a few years an amount of knowledge, and a development of the mental faculties, surprising and even mysterious to him who has never attempted any regular course of self-culture.

And here let me guard you against the too prevalent idea, that mere reading is of itself to benefit you, with little regard to its ultimate scope or design. While, at times, you read simply for amusement and recreation, selecting, of course, such books as are in accordance with the spirit of your faith, — the spirit of purity, benevolence, and truth, — and carefully excluding all such as would vitiate the taste, lower the standard of Christian purity and morality, or degrade the nobler feelings and aspirations of the soul, let such books be read truly as a recreation, while you devote the chief part of your leisure hours to the systematic perusal and study of books that require attention, that will exercise your judgment, test your powers of reason, enlarge your sphere of thought, strengthen the memory, quicken the imagination, and expand the whole intellectual being. Read slowly, and often take notes of what you read. Accustom yourself to writing out, however briefly and simply, your thoughts and opinions on the subjects under discussion. Compare the opinions of different authors, and, in this way, exercise your own judgment; and though you may seemingly accomplish less by pursuing such a course, the true mental acumen thus gained will really be of far more lasting benefit than if dozens of volumes were hastily and carelessly perused.

Do not make it an excuse that you have no time for such pursuits, if hours are spent in devotion to dress, fashion, and amusement. Having consecrated yourself in the secret purpose of the heart to your Master's service, does he not demand of you to render the daily account of this portion of your stewardship,—to prepare yourself by the faithful use of every opportunity, however humble, to exert a higher and wider influence, knowing that the more you are in yourself, the richer and fuller your mental resources, the more you can ever be to others? Might not an hour be sometimes taken from your slumbers, or a dress trimmed less fashionably, or the table spread less luxuriously, or an advantageous bargain less eagerly pursued, in order to attain those enduring riches, that wealth of mind, and that power of thought, which no change can take from you? The unfaithful servant who buried his one talent had even the single gift taken from him; while the promise that more shall be given is pledged alone to him who seeks truly to cultivate and improve every capacity and opportunity, however slight.

If you would be a true disciple, a certain portion of your time is, in some way or form, to be faithfully devoted to others. If pressing home duties and cares do not fully occupy you, — and this is rarely the case if they be rightly and methodically arranged, though, of course, they ever possess the first claim, — then, if you truly desire to follow Christ, you will seek out other paths of effort and usefulness, will cheer the chamber of sickness and the abode of poverty, instruct the young, counsel the ignorant, help the tempted, and reap those rich harvests of charity and love spread all around you. You can also aid others less favorably situated in their intellectual pursuits, and impart of what you have freely received; or by the faithful use of your pen, you can often, in the simple, friendly letter, strengthen the wavering purpose, excite the noble desire, and animate the sluggish spirit to higher and more spiritual aims; for remember that self-consecration to God includes the faithful use of *all* your time, talents, and opportunities.

And here let me guard you against a false balancing of your duties, or a selfish view of your daily routine of business. There is too prevalent among many a sort of busy idleness, that deems itself always occupied, and prides itself upon the amount of labor accomplished. And yet what is the real result? Compared with the Gospel standard, what is its true and ultimate end? Is it worthy the life of an immortal being?

To spend hour after hour, and day after day, in the best season of life, in the use of the needle, where there is no demand for personal maintenance, in mere embroidery, or in seeking to keep up with the constantly changing style of fashion and dress, not content with mere comfort or simple elegance and taste, but indulging in the love of show, display, and overloaded ornament, and then giving the poor excuse, when called upon for any work of kindness or deed of charity, that there is *no time* to attend to such things, —does it not evince a perverse state of the moral character, a heart far distant from the heart of the Redeemer? Do not misunderstand me. Every accomplishment and the cultivation of every taste has its true and rightful place; but are you not bound, in the use of your leisure hours, by your very Christian discipleship, to ask seriously and thoughtfully, "Lord, what wilt *thou* have me to do?" Have you a right to mere self-indulgence and ease, when even Christ pleased not himself, when the Master you have chosen came not to be ministered unto, but to minister? Might not the hour too readily given to work of no real value, to the novel or the mere fashionable call, be far better employed in earnest self-improvement, in efforts for those less advantageously situated, in reading to some weary invalid, or seeking to comfort some stricken and sorrowing spirit? After a day thus passed, would you not lie down to rest at night with a fuller and more peaceful consciousness of having striven, at least, to be faithful in your stewardship, however humble in the world's eye?

So far as the choice of your pursuits lies within your own control, have some due regard to your individual tastes and talents, and never undertake the acquirement of any particular accomplishment simply because it is the fashion. You cannot reasonably expect to excel in all branches and pursuits, and has not God marked out, in a great measure, the true path for each, by their individual gifts and preferences? For instance, to spend hours every day, year after year, at that period when the mind is most active and most receptive, in acquiring a mere mechanical proficiency on some musical instrument, where there is no ear or taste, is little better than an utter waste of time; while the same leisure, pains, and attention, directed to more congenial pursuits, would prepare the individual to exert a far higher influence, and assure to him real wealth of mind and of heart. Remember, too, that such leisure hours, and such seasons of life, when, to a greater or less extent, your time is at your own disposal, are opportunities for which you are sacredly responsible. In the Saviour's teachings the sins of omission are no less severely dealt with than those of commission. "Not every one who saith unto me, Lord, Lord, shall enter into the kingdom of Heaven, but he who *doeth the will* of my Father who is in heaven." "Inasmuch as ye *did it not* to one of the least of these my brethren, ye did it not to me."

Your means of expenditure, whether greater or less, are also to be held as a sacred trust, and never for mere purposes of self-indulgence. If God has placed within your control more than is essential for the mere comforts of life, you are to look upon its use as a stewardship for which you are to render a strict account. And if your consecration of all that you have and are has been full and unreserved, you will not look to the example or fashion of those around you, but again will the earnest inquiry arise in your heart, "Lord, what wilt thou have me to do?"

Adopt a simple, modest style of dress, such as will never attract attention, and let it always be such as is consistent with your means, your individual duties and occupations, and conducive to health and comfort. But to load the dress with superfluous ornaments, to be ever changing the style and fashion, to exercise not the slightest self-denial, to expend all your means in mere selfish indulgence from a vain love of admiration and display, and, when called upon to aid in any work of charity, to reply that you cannot possibly afford it, that you are too poor to give, — does it not evince a spirit little in unison with that of the cross?

Remember, too, that no man liveth to himself, and that the Christian is a living epistle, known and read by all men. While you cast the mantle of charity over others who err in this respect, you cannot but feel in your inmost soul that their personal Christian influence is weakened by such self-indulgence, and such apparent love of display and admiration. And in the hour of secret prayer and confession, must you not often bow in humility, that so many thoughts are given to mere external show and fashion, so much time expended on what must perish with the using?

In the words of another: "Could some magic reflection be added to mirrors, so that, while they show back the adjustment of garments, they should also reveal the emptiness of the soul, what dismal disclosures would startle the sleeping conscience! How slow pride is to learn, that every accumulation of useless finery upon the person bears an exact proportion to the poverty of character beneath it! When the true Christian standard of dress and furnishing shall be confessed, these wasteful outlays on gaudy colors and superfluous ornaments will be blushed for as indecencies. God, in his justice, cannot be satisfied while the grand charities and philanthropies of his kingdom languish, and the treasures of ostentation are so full."

As one who desires to be a disciple of the lowly and humble Redeemer, "let your adorning then be not the outward adorning of plaiting the hair, and of wearing of gold, or of putting on of apparel, but let it be the hidden man of the heart, in that which is not corruptible, even the ornament of a meek and quiet spirit, which is, in the sight of God, of great price."

Remember, too, the Apostle's exhortation, that "whether we eat or drink, or whatsoever we do, we do all to the glory of God"; that is, let every appetite be brought under the control and regulation of Christian principle, and made subject to the great laws of accountability. As in dress so in food and drink, have a regard to the health and well-being of the body, this wonderful instrument through which the soul holds intercourse with the external world; and so use it and care for it, so reverence its wonderful mechanism, and the Divine wisdom and care displayed even in its minutest members, that you may truly render it a pure and fitting temple for the indwelling of the immortal spirit.

Never despise or violate the laws of health and of your physical well-being by vain self-indulgence, carelessness, or mere love of fashion; for so intimate is the connection between the material and the spiritual, that you cannot violate the laws of your bodily organization without feeling surely and necessarily the reaction in sluggish moods, weakened moral and intellectual powers, and crippled efforts for progress and improvement.

In whatever you do, however humble your occupation, however trivial your duties, do *all* to the glory of God. By cheerfulness, punctuality, honesty, fidelity, self-forgetfulness, and forbearance, recommend the truth of Christ to every man's conscience, and evince that not in name alone, but in deed and in heart, you are a disciple of your Master.

Guard your secret springs of thought, check the rising of passion, and hold the temper in faithful subjection. "The temper itself, in fact, is one of the ingredients in our composition most independent of immediate and voluntary control. Control over it is gained by the will only through long and patient discipline; and so it is an effectual revealer of our real selves. It acts so suddenly, that deliberation has not time to dictate its behavior, and, like other tell-tales, it is so much in a hurry, that an after-thought fails to overtake the first message. It lets the hidden man out, and pulls off his mask." Have the mastery, then, over your inward self, and you will never be the prey of changing circumstances or sudden temptation, or exclaim, as so many do, at any unforeseen occurrence: "It was too provoking! it was beyond endurance!" Would it have been beyond the Saviour's endurance and forbearing love? Would his spirit have been kindled in anger at the slight provocation that excites the passionate word?

Is it not, rather, because you have not faithfully learned of Him who was meek and lowly in heart, who, when he was reviled, reviled not again, that so often the blush of anger crimsons your cheek, and the hasty word passes your lips? Only feel that this victory over self, this conquest over temper and passion, *is* possible,—only strive and pray earnestly and daily that your whole soul may be renewed in the Divine image,—and you will surely come off more than conqueror through Him that hath loved us. Only compare your thoughts and words, your feelings and temper, with his pure, gentle, loving, and forgiving spirit, and not with the low standard, and the imperfect attainments, of those around you; and looking into his heavenly countenance, with his eye resting upon you, will you not long and pray to be delivered from every unholy passion, every irritable feeling, every thought even, that shall separate you from a full and entire communion with his pure and spotless spirit?

In great things you do brace yourself for the conflict; but in petty duties and trifling vexations you yield from want of watchfulness and prayer, and anger and impatience too often gain the mastery.

But remember the arena of your conflict. Beneath the eye of the All-holy One, with the hand of the Son of God stretched forth to sustain you, with the secret influences of the Spirit to cheer you on your course, and the crown of life upheld as the reward of the faithful combatant, shall you not press forward with eager zeal and constant watchfulness, even to the attainment of the prize of your high calling?

If toil be thus hallowed by the Father's presence, and duty performed in the Master's spirit, and every trial of patience and of temper made conducive to the soul's eternal growth and progress, will you not learn to look upon the daily life as indeed the appointed means of your spiritual discipline, — the path, rough and broken and steep, it may be, yet the sure and certain path, to lead you to the Father's nearer presence, — to your higher home above?

Let your conversation and your hours of social intercourse be also faithfully regulated and governed by the great laws of Christian truth, forbearance, gentleness, and love. Not alone by deeds are you to manifest your Christian discipleship; but in those hours of unreserved social communion when your words are uttered without restraint, in the home circle, or with a few chosen friends, you are equally to remember your obligation to observe the most exact truth in every statement, and to let your conversation be pervaded and marked by the spirit of Christian charity and love.

Many there are, kind in act and generous in deed, whose words are sharper than a two-edged sword, so that the nearest friend is never sure of escaping the shaft of bitter satire or of keen ridicule. Others delight to utter the secret innuendo, to repeat the last tale of slander or the mere gossip of the neighborhood, and, often without any direct intention of exceeding the limits of truth, by artifices of voice or manner, or by setting the tale in a new light to render it the more effective, enhance or change its import, until as it passes from one to another the plain and real truth is so concealed and distorted as to be wholly beyond recognition. How fruitful are the harvests from such departures from the eternal laws of truth, justice, and love, I need not say. Unkind dissensions, bitter jealousies, petty enmities, alienated families and neighborhoods in every community, bear too evident witness of the prevalence of an evil and sin, indulged in with little or no compunction by many who call themselves Christians.

But if your self-consecration has been true in its aim and purpose, you will keep a strict and watchful guard over your words, and weigh every utterance. Even in the hour of playful conversation or of trifling repartee, you will not forget that the eye of the God of Truth and of Love is upon you; and your words, however gay and light, will yet be uttered as in his presence, and will be free from all scandal, gossip, or unkindness.

In the home circle, let your conversation be cheerful and loving, seeking at fit times to contribute directly to the improvement of those around you; and in the larger social gathering, at the pleasant party, or the joyous feast, remember that even there Christ recognizes his true disciple no less than in the secret closet, — that even there the Master's image is to be faithfully reflected in your soul.

Avoid as you would a deadly poison the base

habit of exaggeration, misstatement, misrepresentation, and petty scandal. Indulge in no remarks about others, and repeat no words of ill-natured gossip, which you would shrink from uttering in the Saviour's presence, or hearing from his lips.

Better, far better, a continued silence, than to gain the reputation of being an entertaining, agreeable person, at the expense of blunting each finer moral feeling, and of violating the laws of truth and of Christian charity.

Were there a thorough reform among Christians even in this single respect, we might expect to enjoy a heaven upon earth, compared with the numerous troubles and dissensions now created by the mere neglect to control the words and sanctify the speech by the spirit of exact and entire truthfulness. And does not habitual indulgence in this so-called petty sin evince a *heart* utterly uncontrolled by true Christian principle, — a spirit that has never really felt its own sinfulness, or realized the Saviour's tender and forbearing love? "Out of the abundance of the heart the mouth speaketh." If you delight in listening to petty scandal, in repeating the tale of slander, in detracting from the merits of your neighbor, in indulging in mean suspicions and covert surmises, be assured there is that *within* which needs a thorough and entire renewal, a spirit unsubdued and unsanctified, a heart that rests not on the Redeemer. "A good tree cannot bring forth evil fruit, neither can a corrupt tree bring forth good fruit; wherefore by their *fruits* ye shall know them."

Remember, too, that you possess no more fruitful opportunities of doing good than in the use you make of your simple, daily words, or of hours of prolonged conversation. How often can you speak the word of encouragement, or roll back the cloud of disappointment, suffering, or anxiety, by a timely expression of love and of sympathy! How often can you bless the heart of childhood, or cheer the lonely spirit, by the utterance of a glad and holy trust! How often can you impart your own treasures of mind and heart to those less favorably situated, or, by a free, spiritual communion, how may another soul be quickened to a nobler, higher life, and inspired with a deeper and more trusting faith! While you never introduce direct religious conversation at unseasonable times or places, let all your words be so pervaded by a truly religious *spirit*, that, whether in a grave or gay, a serious or lively mood, they shall ever mirror the purity of the soul's inmost being, — a purity that would shun even the thought of sin, and is satisfied only as it reflects more and more clearly and distinctly the Divine image.

While you mingle freely with others in the daily duties and business of life and in the social circle, choose for your intimate friends and associates those only who will truly aid you in your spiritual progress, and whose influence and example will tend to excite and quicken your own endeavors. And remember that such true spirits are not confined to any one walk or sphere of life; but that alike in the home of luxury and the abode of poverty you will find the Master's image reflected, by its own inherent attraction ever bringing others within the circle of its gentle and true influence.

> "Our many deeds, the thoughts that we have thought,
> They go out from us, thronging every hour;
> And in them all is folded up a power,
> That on the earth doth move them to and fro;
> And mighty are the marvels they have wrought,
> In hearts we know not, and may never know."

I have thus spoken of the need of unceasing watchfulness and circumspection amid all the duties of the daily life, and have endeavored to show you that the one purpose of self-consecration necessarily includes the Christian use of your time, means, and opportunities, the control of your thoughts and desires, the government of your appetites and passions, the regulation of your speech, and your intercourse with others. I do not ask whether this is an easy attainment. Such a question the Christian pilgrim will never pause to consider, for his only motto ever is, "Upward and onward"; — "Be ye perfect, even as your Father is perfect."

"O watch, and strive, and pray!
The battle ne'er give o'er;
Renew it boldly every day,
And help divine implore.
Ne'er think the victory won,
Nor lay thine armor down;
Thy arduous work will not be done
Till thou obtain thy crown."

Remember, too, that this very discipline of the daily life is the heaven-appointed means, not only of strengthening and purifying the inward nature, but also of testing the true metal of character, and thus showing us our real selves. If we are overcome by slight temptations and yield to petty provocations, — if we are faithless in duty, or hide the truth by mean prevarication or unjust slander, — if temper habitually gain the mastery, and anger flush the brow, — then we may be sure that there is something wrong within, and that mere external remedies and defences will be of no avail. The heart must be anchored by the Rock of Ages, would it breast the storms of sudden temptation and trial, would it rest in peace amid the buffetings of the daily life.

The martyr's faith and courage, and the martyr's endurance, are not qualities to be assumed at the moment of trial, but must have their firm root in faithful struggles and earnest efforts, in sincere convictions, and in victories that have been gained in the secrecy of the inmost soul. The patient forbearance and the calm trust in the midst of anxiety and sorrow, the temper unruffled by provocation and injury, the unwearied fidelity to uncongenial duties, evince ever that the conflict has been waged, and the victory won, through those deep struggles of the spirit known only to the unseen eye.

"I have seen," says another, "a sudden thunder-gust smite an elm on one of our river-meadows, tossing its branches, twisting its trunk, prying at its root until it writhed as if wrestling with an invisible Titan, and tearing off a few light leaves to whirl in airy eddies, but yet struggling in vain to unsettle the firm and elastic lord of the green valley from its place. Did the earth give her graceful and kingly child, as the cloud came up, any special props or braces, any thicker bark or longer root to breast the shock? All these had to be provided in the persevering nurture of spring suns and winter blasts, sap-giving summer nights and dripping autumn rains, when no eye could mark the gradual growth. The tempest did not create the vigor which it tried and proved, and left erect as ever."

Nay, the vigor and the strength must ever come through those silent and secret ministries unnoticed by the outward eye, — through patient toil and faithful self-communion and earnest watchfulness, and that heart-felt prayer which alone can bring the soul into true communion with the unseen and spiritual.

Thus only can you form a true, consistent, noble, generous, Christian character. Thus only can you enter into that higher faith of the soul, which not alone believes, but *trusts* with an unwavering assurance, the Father's promise, and rests in the Saviour's reconciling love. Thus only can you be in heart and in life a faithful, humble, sincere disciple of the Master.

LETTER XIII.

THE SABBATH.

In your last letter, my dear friend, you ask in what way you can best spend the Sabbath, in order to render its hours conducive to your highest spiritual interests. I reply, that, while the manner of passing this sacred time must necessarily vary with individual circumstances and needs, there are certain great ends to be kept in view, to be modified according to your own views of duty and responsibility.

We speak of the seventh day as a season of rest; but let me earnestly entreat you not to fall into the habit, too common among many, of rendering it a day devoted to mere bodily repose, ease, and sloth, — a day to indulge in the prolonged morning slumber, to enjoy the luxurious repast, to attend the public services of religion once indeed as a sort of bane to conscience, but to return home and while away the remaining hours by discussing the latest news, by frivolous and idle conversation, or dissipating every serious impression made at church by giving the succeeding hours to the letter of mere gossip, or to the last new novel or popular magazine of the day. How is it possible to unite in the worship of the sanctuary, and join in the prayers and praises of the house of God, with any degree of fervor and interest, if the preceding hours have been given solely to dress, trifling conversation, or light reading? How can one expect to feel any interest in the simple services of the Church, or to find them the means of spiritual growth, if no preparation has been made for receiving the truth, and no earnest need or desire felt for Divine light and guidance? Were the secret thoughts of each heart clearly laid open, as from Sabbath to Sabbath we meet avowedly for the worship of Jehovah, for communion with the Master and Saviour, and unitedly to supplicate the holy influences of the Spirit, what strange, what humiliating disclosures would startle us from our dull indifference, our vain and trifling thoughts, our earth-bound desires! To how many would the service prove a mere form of outward decency, with no heart and no soul; and how many would be found to regard it wholly as a sort of intellectual stimulus, and, if this were wanting, would pronounce it at once dull, indifferent, and worthless!

We cannot, it is true, expect to feel an equal interest in every service of public worship; but if there has been the preparation of the heart, the secret communion, the hour of retirement and prayer, there are few occasions when the soul may not derive new strength, quickening, and fervor from uniting with others in acts of social prayer and praise. Do not complain that such hours are of no availing benefit to you, so long as you have not been faithful on *your* part. Prepare the soul for the service by turning the thoughts inward, and striving to realize more deeply your secret wants and needs, by gaining wider views of your duty, and letting your spirit mount in earnest prayer and aspiration in view of your immortal destiny; or bending in lowly humility and confession, rest at the foot of the cross, and seek there the pardon, strength, and help you need. And returning from the service of united confession and thanksgiving, deepen the impressions made by reviewing what you have heard, and turning your thoughts to subjects of a kindred nature. Occasionally take notes of the sermon to which you have listened, especially if it has been one that has peculiarly interested or impressed you, and in this way deepen the impressions made, until the truths uttered become strong and abiding convictions in your soul, — a part of your very life and being.

The Sabbath was, indeed, made for man a day of rest, but was made for him that it might be the rest of progress, the rest derived from change of pursuits and occupations, the rest of earnest endeavors and spiritual communings, the rest of laboring for others and contributing to their happiness and improvement.

Make it emphatically a day for spiritual thought, communion, and prayer, — a day for gaining higher ideas of duty and progress, for bringing you into closer fellowship with the unseen world, for leading you nearer to God, to Christ, and to heaven. However you may be situated, endeavor sacredly to set apart some portion of its hours for private meditation and prayer, for learning more truly your own spiritual wants and needs, and for obtaining a more vital faith in those helps and blessings ever promised to the sincere seeker.

Let your reading be such as will advance your spiritual life, quicken each sluggish endeavor, elevate your thoughts, ennoble your aspirations, strengthen you for duty and effort, and bring you into a closer harmony with all that is pure, true, and heavenly. Make the Bible your first and chief study; and in saying this I feel that I am opening before you a field of inquiry and research, which will more than occupy every leisure Sabbath hour. Study it in the spirit of humility and prayer; study it, first and chief of all, for its rich, spiritual truths, and with a faithful individual application to your own needs; but remember that you are also sacredly bound to gain as thorough and complete an intellectual knowledge of this divine record as lies in your power, — of the evidences of its truth, the history of its various books, the manner of its compilation, the wonderful fortunes of the chosen race, the influence both of Judaism and Christianity upon the advance of civilization and the progress of higher truths among mankind.

However brief may be the time you are able to devote to such pursuits during the week, one or two hours only, faithfully devoted to such a course of inquiry on each Sabbath, would impart to you an amount of knowledge and an increased power of thought, the value of which you can hardly over-estimate.

Then you have the rich stores of Christian biography, from which you can draw so many incentives to duty, and which so eminently tend to quicken the inner life, and rouse the soul to higher purposes and efforts. Only keep distinctly in view the one great end of rendering the day a season of spiritual progress, of making its hours subservient to your highest religious interests, and your own judgment will point out to you the true path; remembering that you are to have regard to the influence of your example over others in this respect, no less than in the duties and business of the daily life.

You have, too, spread all around you the wonderful displays of the Divine power and goodness in the works of creation, and, turning from the written page, let your thoughts rest in grateful adoration upon the love and wisdom of Him who unfolds before you the constantly changing book of nature, and offers to your inquiring glance such rich treasures of spiritual thought and wealth.

And do not vainly imagine that it is essential for you to possess, as some, the privilege of visiting places of renown, — the snow-crowned mountain, the thundering cataract, the bald ocean cliff, the placid lake of surpassing loveliness, — in order truly to enjoy and enter into the deep spiritual meaning of the rich beauty which the Father's hand has spread all around us. Not partially, as man, does He bestow the gifts of his bounty. However confined and circumscribed the limits of your home may be, day follows day and night succeeds to night in their ceaseless alternation of light and of darkness, and "there is no speech nor language where *their* voice is not heard." The sky overarches you in its solemn grandeur, its ceaseless change of beauty and glory, and there is not a single hour when, if you turn your eye in wondering adoration above, you cannot there discern the very finger of the Almighty, displaying, as in no other form, the inexhaustible riches of his own infinite spirit of loveliness and grandeur.

"The sky is as a temple's arch;
The blue and wavy air

Is glorious with the spirit-march
Of messengers at prayer.

"The gentle moon, the kindling sun,
The many stars, are given,
As shrines to burn earth's incense on,
The altar-fires of heaven."

Even the simple blade of grass at your door, now bathed with the morning dew, now sparkling in the clear sunshine, and now reflecting a darker hue, as the passing cloud or the o'erhanging bough shields it from the noonday sun, speaks in ever-living tones of the love and care of Him who listens to the faintest whisper of the child's heart. The wild-flowers of field and forest, the soft, green moss, the mountain lichen, the barky trunk, the fresh, moist ground of spring, the delicate tendrils of the simple vine as it climbs around your very door,— are not all instinct with the spirit of a Power, Beauty, and Love ever around and ever near you? And in the light of the Saviour's teachings, in the light reflected from his broken sepulchre, in the holy remembrances of that "first day of the week," do not the most common scenes of nature become transfigured with a new and wonderful glory?

The very heavens become radiant with a deeper beauty, as we remember how they were parted over the Jordan, and the baptism of the Holy One was sealed by those Divine words,

"This is my beloved Son"; and a holier light is reflected from each placid stream and sparkling wave, as they speak to the soul of those waters of which he who drinketh shall never thirst, — as they become symbolical of that river, "the streams whereof make glad the city of our God." Even the gathering mists and the dark and lowering clouds become transfused with a brighter glow, as we listen to the voice that spake amid the storm, and hushed the raging waters, saying, "Peace, be still." And when, in some favored hour, we gaze on the wide amphitheatre of forests, hills, and mountains, a sublimer beauty and a holier majesty crown their summits, as they remind us of those everlasting hills, "from whence cometh our help," — that, "as the mountains are round about Jerusalem, so the Lord is round about them that fear him," — as we remember those once with us, now beholding the glories of the New Jerusalem, the city "that hath no need of the sun or the moon to shine in it, for the glory of God doth lighten it, and the Lamb is the light thereof."

Consecrated by such a spirit, will you not find in the works of nature a new and inexhaustible fountain of spiritual truth and power, a medium through which you can ever hold communion with your Father and your Saviour?

A portion of your Sabbath, if its hours are in any measure under your own control, should also be set apart for the direct instruction of others, the young or the ignorant, either in your own home or in the Sabbath school. As you have received, so are you sacredly bound to impart of your own spiritual advantages and blessings; and in no way can you more truly deepen and quicken your inward being, than by seeking to aid others in walking in the narrow path of life. Give, freely and fully, even though it be at the cost of some sacrifice of ease and indulgence. Deem it a privilege, if in any form or way you can labor in your Master's vineyard, if you can follow him in his walks of benevolence and labors of love. Be faithful to your high calling as a Christian disciple, and the Sabbath will never be a weariness, but a period blessed above other seasons for its privileges and opportunities, its hours for direct spiritual communion, for secret meditation and social worship,—its hours both for receiving and imparting the truths revealed through the mission and mediation of a crucified and risen Saviour. Let it be a day of cheerfulness and of quiet joy,—a day when the ordinary pursuits of life are laid aside, and its hours especially consecrated to the worship of God, to the cultivation of the religious nature, and to the use of such means as shall fit the soul the better to meet the trials and discipline of the daily life, and prepare it more truly for that direct, spiritual communion and intercourse

in the Master's society promised to the faithful servant.

A Sabbath thus passed will bring with it its own special blessings ; and in a deeper religious faith, in larger powers of usefulness, in more spiritual endeavors and aims, and a more faithful walk among men, you will reap the blessed effects of its hours of holy consecration and prayer.

May you so improve these hours, that they will indeed be to you a foretaste of your heavenly home, of an eternal Sabbath of progress and of joy.

"Then shall a new, a spirit childhood come,
A fresher sense of life in thee have room !
A life that knows no pain, no death, no tomb !
There sight shall know what faith hath first believed ;
There perfect trust thy heart hath ne'er conceived ;
There sadd'ning thoughts be gone, thy mind here grieved !
Then for the work, my soul, that waits thee there,
A firm, bold heart within thee daily bear,
Undimmed by painful thoughts, unbowed by care."

LETTER XIV.

THE CHURCH OF CHRIST.

It has been with deep interest, my dear friend, that I have watched your progress in the spiritual life, and your earnest endeavors to be a true disciple of your Saviour and Redeemer. But while you are striving to govern your inward being, and to regulate your daily life by his teachings and example, let me ask if one thing is not still wanting as an aid to your own spiritual progress and consecration, and needful to give to your example and influence its due and rightful efficacy.

While you have consecrated yourself in the secrecy of your own heart to your Master's service, and are seeking to become more and more conformed to his spirit and to look to him as your only Saviour, is there not an obligation laid upon you by the very name you wish to bear of a Christian disciple, to observe the simple ordinances of his appointment, and in outward rite to confirm the resolve and the dedication made before God in your own soul? Remembering him who came from the bosom of the Father, leaving the glory which he had with him before the world was, being baptized with the baptism of sorrow and of suffering, and crucified that we might live, will you longer hesitate openly and fully to acknowledge having chosen him as your Lord and Master? Feeling your dependence upon God's mercy in him as your only refuge and strength, will you refuse to sit at his table of commemorative love, and, in the ordinance of his own appointment, to remember him, your Saviour and Intercessor?

If, in early infancy, you were dedicated to your Father and your Saviour by holy parental love, then renew now in the sanctuary of your own heart, and take upon yourself, those vows of consecration, and come and openly call yourself a disciple of your Master, by remembering him in his feast of dying love.

But if the emblematic water has never rested upon your brow, typical of that inward purity to which the Christian disciple aspires, of that cleansing from all the defilements of sin and of evil for which he prays and longs through the influences of the Spirit, then remember the Saviour's own example, when the voice came from the open heavens, "This is my beloved Son, hear ye him"; remember his parting words, "Go ye into all the world and preach the Gospel to every creature, baptizing them in the name of the Father, and of the Son, and of the Holy Ghost."

Observe the rite, not as a mere form, not as an act possessing some peculiar or magic efficacy, but as one by which you recognize your relation to the Church of Christ, by which you bring yourself into membership with that great spiritual body of which he is the head, by which you express your inward desire and purpose to be henceforward freed from the stains of sin, and to become pure and holy, reflecting in your soul the Master's image. Observe it in the spirit of humility and prayer, feeling assured that in your own strength you are nothing and can do nothing, but that through Christ aiding you, you can do all things. Go, too, to the Lord's table, and in penitence and lowliness, yet with a hopeful, trusting spirit, remember him who has so faithfully aided you thus far, and who has promised ever to abide with you and to dwell within you; remember him who suffered that you might live; and watching with him in that shaded garden of agony, and standing beside that cross of suffering and of shame, can you coldly turn away, and feel no wish to take part in his festival of redeeming love?

As your weary, anxious spirit has found repose in his tenderness and sympathy; as the burden of care and duty has become lightened through his sustaining love and guidance; as the clouds of sorrow and grief have been fringed with rays of heavenly light from his countenance; as the sin-burdened, alienated heart has been brought back to its Father through his divine ministry of reconciliation, pardon, and peace; as every glad and joyous scene has been doubly blessed by his smile of love, — have you no acknowledgment to make of what he has done, and is even now doing, for your soul?

In your own heart calling him Master and Saviour, will you longer hesitate openly and truly to express that consecration and faith in the ordinances of his own appointment? Will it not be both a sacred duty and a blessed privilege?

Not high attainments, not a mature experience, does he demand; but the simple wish and the sincere purpose to be his humble and faithful disciple. "Come unto me, for he that cometh I will in no wise cast out." It is not the voice of your friend, nor that of any human being, that appeals to you, but that of the Son of God. He presides at the feast; his voice bids all to come to him who would choose him as their Master and Guide, — all who have any love to him, or who sincerely long to love him more truly, and to serve him more faithfully.

Not those who feel that they have attained, or are already perfect, does he invite to take part in that service of love; but the heart longing to be his, the spirit striving for progress, that would fain rest in his bosom of redeeming love, — the soul conscious of sin and weakness, yet humbly hoping and trusting for forgiveness and redemption from all sin through his love and reconciling mercy.

As you now stand, your position lacks firm ness and definiteness. There is either such a thing as a Church, or there is not; and by the Church I mean that body of individuals, of whatever creed, nation, or clime, who believe in Jesus as the Son of God and the Saviour of men, and who so believe in him as to be desirous, above all things else, of leading his spiritual life, and of being spiritually united to him. It is that body of Christian believers of which Christ is literally and spiritually the Head. According to the teachings of our Saviour and his Apostles, the one distinguishing *sign* of admission to the Church is the rite of baptism, administered either to the child or the adult; in the former case, the parents, of course, solemnly pledging themselves to educate the child as a member of that Church, and to make the relation as true and real to him as that which he holds to the family circle, — a relation which he will gladly recognize for himself in maturer years, for he will feel that he is a child of the Church no less than a child of earthly parents, and his earnest desire will be to prove himself a faithful disciple of his Saviour.

So of the Lord's Supper. The teachings of the Apostles, and all Christian history, point out this ordinance as a direct, voluntary, positive, and outward recognition of a church relation. However observed, at whatever times, or with whatever confession, its simple observance is expressive of love, gratitude, and consecration to the Master, — of the desire to enter into a closer and more spiritual relation to him, who has promised ever to abide with the sincere and seeking soul. In the words of another: "As Baptism signifies the washing away of former sins, and is the emblem of repentance, so partaking of the Supper signifies a taking of the bread which cometh down from heaven, the being nourished in Christian, spiritual life, and is thus the emblem of Christian growth or holy living. . . . . One thing is here essential, — that we do, in some way, at some time, by some mode of allegiance, acknowledge the Church as an institution or power in the world, having a body and a spirit, of which Christ is directly and personally the Head. Otherwise it is almost superfluous to say one cannot be a Church man or woman. I must not merely say, 'I believe it,' not acting accordingly, and thus practically denying my belief. I must take a *Church position*, and must show my loyalty by service, faith, trust, and deeds."

Hesitate, then, no longer. Come unto Him

whom you have chosen as your Master, and in these ordinances of Divine appointment acknowledge openly Him whom you serve. Come and receive freely the blessings he stands ready to bestow upon every open, fearless disciple, and let no thought or fear of man stand between your soul and its Redeemer. Come, and so confess him before men, that he may confess you before the Father and his holy angels.

Remember, too, that as you take this open, definite position, you express your faith in that vital union which should ever exist between the soul and its Redeemer. "I am the vine, ye are the branches"; and as the abiding and sustaining Comforter, Quickener, and Friend, he has promised to dwell within you, to guide and animate you, to prompt you to duty, to restrain you from sin, to lead you to the Father. You express, too, not merely your affection and allegiance to Christ, but your purpose to strive to be like him, "the willing servant of every human want," — to be prompt in duty, ready for every benevolent exertion, willing to make sacrifices, to give yourself to his work, wherever and however he may point the way.

> "O, give to Christ alone thy heart,
> Thy faith, thy love supreme;
> Then for his sake thine alms impart,
> And so give *all* to him."

But you say, "At times I feel thus, and would

be willing to make any exertion or sacrifice; but again I am cold and indifferent, and I dare not trust my own faith and purposes." I reply, that if you are conscious of *sincerity* of purpose and aim, of having made the distinct choice of Christ as your Saviour and Guide, then observe these very ordinances which he has appointed as *means* of spiritual nourishment, growth, and quickening. God reads your heart, and, while your feelings may often vary according to your peculiar temperament and the influence of outward circumstances, He knows the settled purpose, the true and real desire, of the inmost soul. While, then, you may not always be able to feel the same fervor and interest, let the observance of the holy Supper be preceded by self-examination and prayer, by communion with your Saviour, and meditation on all that he has done, and has promised to do, for you, and it will never be without some quickening, hallowing power over your soul. If observed in a right spirit, it will be the means of greater watchfulness, of a truer earnestness, and a more faithful walk among men; weaving stronger bonds of spiritual union, and bringing you into closer harmony with the great Head of the Church Universal.

Come, then, and in these ordinances of Divine appointment openly and joyfully acknowledge your relationship to Christ, your membership in the one great spiritual Church of which he is the

Life and the Head. Consecrate yourself to the Father who loves you, who has ever watched over, kept, and sustained you, — the God of eternal wisdom, power, and love. Consecrate yourself to your Saviour, to him who lived and died for you, who has given you the assurance of pardon and salvation through his redeeming love, who has promised to aid you, and to dwell with and in you, even as your spirit turns to him in humble faith for strength and blessing. Consecrate yourself to those influences of the Holy Spirit promised, through Christ, to every believing, waiting soul; and thus acknowledging your Divine allegiance before men, thus confessing your Saviour on earth, may you be aided so to live, that he shall at length receive you, a redeemed and purified spirit, to his nearer presence, — that you may hear his own joyous words of welcome, "Well done, good and faithful servant! enter thou into the joy of thy Lord!"

LETTER XV.

THE HOME OF THE BELIEVER.

SINCE I last wrote to you, my dear friend, you have been called to pass through new and trying experiences, in the removal from your little circle of one very near and dear to you. Another has passed on, leaving your home solitary indeed, yet leaving the blessed memories of her pure and Christ-like spirit to cheer and guide you, as you strive, through earnest prayer and a trusting faith, to say with your Redeemer, "Father, thy will, not mine, be done!" "If ye loved me, ye would rejoice, because I go unto the Father"; and while the discipline of this present life is needed for your further purification, needed to prepare you better for those higher and wider spheres of progress and of love in the Saviour's immediate presence, will you not, even amid your sorrow, listen to those blessed words: "I am the Resurrection and the Life; in my Father's house are many mansions, — I go to prepare a place for you; and if I go and prepare a place for you, I will come again, and receive you unto myself, that where I am, there ye may be also"? Will you not turn with a deeper faith to Him who has taught us, by his own cross as well as by his lips, that *through* suffering the soul is made perfect, — made strong, patient, trustful? Will you not look upon this new bereavement as one of those marks of favor, honor, and distinction, which the Father, who loveth those whom He chasteneth, has set upon you? What hearts so likely to preserve the elevation, peace, and strength of the spiritual life, as those which have some of their nearest friends already within the veil, dwelling among things unseen to these mortal eyes? In what spirits is prayer likely to be so fervent, and the daily life so true, as where the communion of saints is felt to be a precious reality, and the intercourse between earth and heaven is innocently kept open and free by the passage of human sympathies and affections? What so animating as the thought of the "cloud of witnesses"?

The demands laid on you are now peculiarly strong; yet this is not your burden, but your dignity, not your hardship, but your joy, designed to stimulate and animate, not to depress you. Of yourself you are not sufficient for them, but all the more must you lean on the Almighty arm, and watch for the leadings of His providence. Leave every day to the God who watches over you, cares for you, and will direct your path, and feel that, however desolate your home, he has yet a work for you to fulfil both for yourself and others.

How often in the common routine of life do the things of earth and of time gain an all-absorbing hold upon the mind, while those that are unseen and eternal fade in the dim distance! How often do we forget our entire dependence upon the Father, and imagine that in our own strength we can do and bear all things! How often does the Saviour's love and help and tender sympathy become a mere abstraction, as we vainly rely on human supports, or trust in human sympathy alone! But God, in his infinite mercy, leaves us not to ourselves. He sees our peculiar needs, and, through his own discipline of love, again and again does he seek to lead us nearer to himself; to cause us to rest in him with a faith so full, so true, so entire, that it shall rather be the expression of a full and joyous trust, of that entire submission of the will which ceases to question and to speculate, though it sees no way of deliverance, or meets only a cross.

Well has another said: "While the chief energy of the spiritual life *seems* to be in exercise, in contests with rebellious passions, it is a higher energy that awes them into silence, — it is a diviner strength acting in the hours of the soul's peace than in its seasons of warfare. Its repose is the serene strength of God."

"In the furnace God may prove thee,
Thence to bring thee forth more bright;
But can never cease to love thee, —
Thou art precious in his sight.
God is with thee, —
God, thine everlasting light."

As in sorrow and sadness, yet with an un questioning faith, you pray for entire submission to the Father's will, will you not feel a deeper gratitude and a holier love to Him, who, through his own resurrection, has given the full assurance of a life over which death can have no power? Will not the desolation of the earthly household lead you to turn a more longing eye to our only true and enduring home? Will it not quicken your hours of devotion, render prayer more fervent, faith more hallowed, and awaken a deeper sympathy towards those suffering under any forms of sorrow or trial?

And if such be its blessed influence, will you shrink from bearing your Master's cross, if thereby you can participate more fully in his spirit, and be drawn nearer the Father?

"Love thou the path of sorrow that Christ trod;
Toil on, and wait in patience for thy rest;
O city of our God! we soon shall see
Thy glorious walls, — home of the loved and blessed."

How does the messenger of sorrow ever bear to the faithful spirit the richest blessings of trust and hope! Not alone do we remain to fulfil our appointed pilgrimage; for there are forms

around us which the outward eye sees not, and we listen to the sound of gentle voices which the outward ear hears not. They come to us in our moments of temptation and trial, and whisper of strength and victory and progress; they hold converse with the spirit in hours of solitude and sadness, and breathe peace and hope into the soul; and as they pass hence, they leave behind them, as Elijah of old, their own rich mantles of power and love. So there are a thousand joyous things in life unheeded when all seems bright around us; but when the calm stream of prayer is supplied by sorrow and disappointment, new beauties and higher thoughts are revealed, and the faithful, simple performance of duty itself, in its triumph over mere feeling, brings its own deep reward and chastened joy.

And how beautifully to the spirit-eye do the most common scenes of life become transformed through the power of death! The places where those whom we love were wont to dwell are henceforth invested with a more sacred influence, and, to the earnest and thoughtful spirit, there comes the voice bidding the soul bow down in reverence, for the spot on which it stands is holy ground. So does every new departure of those whom we love — the faithful disciples of the Master — make the home that is preparing for us more beautiful; for the Saviour has taught us that death is but an incident, and not even a transforming incident, to the spirit. " They wait to receive us with the same countenance of affection they wore upon earth, but more lovely, more radiant, more spiritual. The far country towards which we journey seems nearer to us, and the way less dark; for some have gone before, passing so quietly to their rest that day itself dies not more calmly."

" Though death his sacred seal hath set
 On bright and bygone hours,
Still they we mourn are with us yet,
 Are more than ever ours ; —
Ours by the pledge of love and faith,
 By hopes of heaven on high,
By trust, triumphant over death,
 In immortality."

We read in ancient story that Cleombrotus, a Grecian youth, having read Plato's argument on the immortality of the soul, was so ravished by his descriptions of a future life, that, unwilling to wait nature's dull course, he leaped into the sea, the sooner to be assured of the certainty of his hopes and anticipations.

To him the worth and dignity of this present life were unknown; but will not a true Christian hope unite both worlds, and cause the bow of God's love to encompass both in its beautiful embrace? Not to the sluggish and indifferent spirit are the rich consolations of immortality unfolded; not by undervaluing the present existence are we to learn to prize the glories yet to be revealed. Unless it be Christ for us to *live*, it *cannot* be gain for us to die. Then alone shall we be fully conscious of that "perfect love that casteth out fear"; for only the spirit that sees the Father's hand in the trials as well as in the happiness, in the sorrows no less than in the joys of life, can possess that inward assurance which has power to transform the "reaper whose name is Death" into the angel messenger from the Father.

Such a faith, triumphant in life, the daily, active, busy life of each day, in its toil and its rest, its public business and its hours of retirement, its struggles, hopes, fears, and aspirations, — such a faith, vital, living, ever growing deeper, purer, and more fervent, as it passes through "the trivial round and common task" of daily duty, — such a faith can alone teach us the deep and holy meaning of those sublime words, "Whosoever liveth and believeth in me shall *never* die."

Remember, then, — and let the thought be more and more deeply impressed upon your mind by all the varied discipline of life, — remember that this earth is not your abiding-place, nor this world your home. The spirit that abides in Christ, the heart that rests in the Father's love, the soul whose deepest longings and truest desires are fixed on things unseen and eternal, truly as it rejoices in all that is fair and beauti ful here unfolded to view, will yet ever yearn for that closer fellowship, that holier communion, and that more entire redemption from sin, to be found only in the blessedness, the joy, and peace of its heavenly inheritance.

The Christian's Home! To be with the Father, — no cloud of doubt, no unforgiven sin, to hide the brightness of his unveiled presence, but with a child-like spirit to trust for ever his mercy, truth, and love; to be with Christ, the Saviour of the soul, the sympathizer and helper in every trial and sorrow of the earthly life, to rest in his reconciling love, and to have him still as the Shepherd and Guide among the green pastures and beside the still waters of the Paradise of God; to meet with apostles and prophets, and with the true and holy of every age; to rejoin the loved of our own home circles who have preceded us thither, and who wait to receive us with a deeper and purer affection than when we dwelt with them on earth; to have all fear and sin cast out by perfect love; to join the great company of the redeemed in ascribing "Blessing and honor and glory and power unto Him that sitteth upon the throne, and unto the Lamb," — is not this *home*, the Believer's only true home? "Blessed are they that do his commandments, that they may have right to the tree of life, and may enter in through the gates into the city. And the city had no need of the sun, neither of the moon, to shine in it; for the glory of God did lighten it, and the Lamb is the light thereof."

"My Father's house on high!
Home of my soul, how near
At times, to faith's aspiring eye,
Thy golden gates appear!

"Here in the body pent,
Absent from thee I roam;
Yet nightly pitch my moving tent
A day's march nearer home.

"Be thou at my right hand,
Then can I never fail;
Uphold thou me, and I shall stand;
Help, and I must prevail."

THE END.

www.ingramcontent.com/pod-product-compliance
Lightning Source LLC
LaVergne TN
LVHW011235110826
845150LV00006B/1645

* 9 7 8 1 4 2 5 5 1 3 9 7 9 *